Imperium Press was founded in 2018 to supply students and laymen with works in the history of rightist thought. If these works are available at all in modern editions, they are rarely ever available in editions that place them where they belong: outside the liberal weltanschauung. Imperium Press' mission is to provide right thinkers with authoritative editions of the works that make up their own canon. These editions include introductions and commentary which place these canonical works squarely within the context of tradition, reaction, and counter-Enlightenment thought—the only context in which they can be properly understood.

The Populist Delusion

NEEMA PARVINI

PERTH
IMPERIUM PRESS
2022

Published by Imperium Press

www.imperiumpress.org

FIRST EDITION

A catalogue record for this
book is available from the
National Library of Australia

ISBN 978-1-922602-44-2 Paperback
ISBN 978-1-922602-45-9 Hardcover
ISBN 978-1-922602-46-6 EPUB
ISBN 978-1-922602-47-3 Kindle

CONTENTS

The Populist Delusion

Chapter I
INTRODUCTION

This is a book about the realities of power and how it functions, stripped of all ideological baggage. It has at its core a thesis, which absolutely contradicts the democratic or populist delusion, that the people are or ever could be sovereign. An organised minority always rules over the majority. Perhaps as a testament to that fact, a recent empirical study showed that public opinion has a near-zero impact on law-making in the USA across 1,779 policy issues.[1] In fact, my thesis goes further than that to suggest that all social change at all times and in all places has been top-down and driven by elites rather than 'the people'. Those movements which have the appearance of being organic and bottom-up protests—for example, the 1960s Civil Rights movement in the USA or the Russian Revolutions of 1917—were, in fact, tightly organised and funded by elites. Those attempts to drive change from the 'bottom-up', which is to say, in the absence of elite organisation—we might think of the events of 6th January 2020 in Washington DC or the recent Yellow Vest movement in France—will amount to little more than an inchoate rabble. This principle holds true regardless of the size of the political unit, be that a small company of twenty people, a large organization of thousands of people, a nation of millions, or

1   Martin Gilens and Benjamin I. Page, 'Testing Theories of American Politics: Elites, Interest Groups, and Average Citizens', *Perspectives on Politics*, 12:3 (September 2014), pp. 564–81.

even the entire world. It holds true not only in terms of hard political power—the ability to capture and hold office—but also in two other crucial respects. First, there is the question of logistical power—simply the ability to execute orders—for it is possible to capture office without achieving the ability to execute, as Donald Trump showed. Second, there is the question of the 'soft power' of discourse, of information flow, and of opinion formation.

In addition to democratic delusions, there are also four liberal delusions that will be subject to significant attack by the thinkers who we will be considering. Let us call these the 'Four Myths of Liberalism':

1. *Myth of the stateless society*: that state and society were or could ever be separate.

2. *Myth of the neutral state*: that state and politics were or could ever be separate.

3. *Myth of the free market*: that state and economy were or could ever be separate.

4. *Myth of the separation of powers*: that competing power centres can realistically endure without converging.

In the cold light of reality, these four myths turn out to be little more than wishful thinking.

Before continuing, it is worth emphasising what 'top-down' or 'elite-driven' change means. These phrases may suggest shadowy organisations that puppeteer unseen from the side lines, but that is not the sense in which they should be understood. Rather, the *defining* feature of 'top-down', as opposed to bottom-up, change is the fact of tight minority organization as against the disorganized masses. 'Elite' in this sense could be the elites in currently power or a set of 'counter-elites' who seek to supplant them. In the former case, we could cite examples such as the Civil Rights movement of the 1960s, various LGBT movements, Black Lives Matter or Greta Thunberg and Extinction Rebellion. In these cases, the current power structure uses its considerable influence and resources – whether through legal means using the formal structure of the state and its apparatuses (education, state-backed media, etc) or through non-government organizations (NGOs) and corporate lobby groups – to manufacture consent and *give the appearance* of popular support for elite projects.[2] In the latter case, however, the efforts of counter-elites will only find success in a revolution. As outlined in Chapter 7, revolutions only occur when the current ruling class loses its ability and resolve to maintain power, which will produce widespread popular discontent, *and* when a counter-elite is ready to seize the initiative to fill the vacuum. 'Rebellions happen; revolutions are made'.[3] The superior and tight organization of the counter-elite group determines largely why it is *that* group as opposed to any other that will now take the reins of power. Historical studies on revolutionary figures as diametrically opposed as Vladimir Lenin and Adolf Hitler have noted *tight organizational ability* and *iron discipline* as the defining characteristics of their respective vanguards. Lenin had 'a profound mistrust of the revolutionary potential of the masses, who he believed, without the leadership of an elite party vanguard, would inevitably become diverted by the bread-and-butter issues of Economism.'[4] Likewise, Arthur Bryant described Hitler's NSDAP as

2   This process has been outlined at length by Scott Howard in *The Transgender Industrial Complex* (Quakertown, PA: Antelope Hill, 2020) and *The Open Society Playbook* (Quakertown, PA: Antelope Hill, 2021) and by Kerry Bolton in *Revolution from Above: Manufacturing Dissent in the New World Order* (London: Artkos, 2021) and *The Perversion of Normality: From the Marquis de Sade to Cyborgs* (London: Artkos, 2021). For a much shorter piece, I outline this process in 'Culture is Downstream from Law', *The Forbidden Texts* (5 February 2022): https://forbiddentexts.substack.com/p/culture-is-downstream-from-law.
3   Richard Pipes, *The Russian Revolution* (New York: Vintage Books, 1990), p. 121
4   Orlando Figes, *A People's Tragedy: The Russian Revolution 1891-1924* (London: Pimlico, 1996), p. 152.

'a fighting movement of flawless discipline, and animated by the same unquestioning devotion to its faith and leaders as the old Prussian Guard.' Bryant goes on, 'It must place him among the great organisers of mankind that he was able to establish it so quickly.'[5] Aside from this iron discipline in organization, Lenin and Hitler also had in common an utter contempt for democracy, which was seen as a time-wasting impediment to effective decision-making, and a total disdain for the polite and respectable 'bourgeois' society of the status quo they each sought to supplant. The important point for this study, however, is that neither the rise of the Bolsheviks nor the rise of the Nazis was a *popular uprising* but rather the result of the determined organized efforts of counter-elites. Likewise, the movements of Civil Rights, LGBT rights, Black Lives Matter and Extinction Rebellion were not *popular uprisings* either, but the result of the determined organized efforts of the elites currently in power or, if you prefer, the ruling class.

This book will start by introducing the core tenets of the elite theorists, Gaetano Mosca (Chapter 2), Vilfredo Pareto (Chapter 3) and Robert Michels (Chapter 4). These thinkers give us the indispensable tools and vocabulary with which to analyse politics and power. It will then add crucial insights from two other important political theorists, Carl Schmitt (Chapter 5) and Bertrand de Jouvenel (Chapter 6), to think more about how power and law function *in practice* and about how political change—'the circulation of elites'—can come about. Three chapters will follow on the 'managerial class'—the vital second stratum of the elites or ruling class identified by the elite theories—and the special treatment given to this topic by James Burnham (Chapter 7), Samuel T. Francis (Chapter 8) and Paul Gottfried (Chapter 9). Chapter 10 forms a brief conclusion applying some of these lessons to the current political moment.

It is worth mentioning here that this book is interested

5   Arthur Bryant, *Unfinished Victory* (London: Macmillan, 1940), pp. 236-7.

primarily in the fundamental concepts rooted in these works and not, for example, the lives and contexts of the authors or how their work has been received by scholars over the decades. I will do my best to draw on the vast body of secondary literature, but purely for the purposes of better illustrating the core ideas rather than critiquing them except where necessary. There are two key reasons for this, one practical and the other pedagogical. The former is simply because of space, one could easily write a whole book on each of the chapter topics. The latter, however, is to avoid confusion. Many of the thinkers we are discussing were severely critical of, or even outright hostile to, both socialism and liberal democracy, while many of the scholars who have worked on them have been either socialists or defenders of liberal democracy. Thus, their *purposes* for taking on these thinkers were usually in the service of defending their ideology, whether by re-interpreting or trying to co-opt the thinker for it or trying to find ways to disprove the thinker to 'save' it. This is not to say that any of the scholars in question were dishonest, or that their work was 'bad', or even that their arguments were incorrect, but rather to recognise that they were working in conditions in which they felt the need to pay lip service to the official doctrines—the 'political formulas'—of the status quo. I feel no such obligation. Besides, as John Higley has pointed-ed out, the march of history continues utterly in defiance of democrats and social radicals:

> Many democrats and social radicals have rejected the early elite theorists' 'futility thesis'.[6] They have sought to demonstrate that particular elites are not those with superior endowments or organizational capacities, but merely persons who are socially advantaged in power competitions. Adherents of this view have argued that the existence of elites can be terminated either by removing the social advantages that some

6   Joseph V. Femia, *Against the Masses: Varieties of Anti-Democratic Thought since the French Revolution* (Oxford: Oxford University Press, 2001), p. 67.

> people enjoy or by abolishing the power concentra-
> tions that spur competitions among them—remedies
> that often go hand-in-hand. There are no historical
> instances, however, where these remedies have been
> successfully applied in a large population for any sig-
> nificant length of time.[7]

This book seeks to advance a value-free analysis which is not in the service of any ideology. If power in human societies functions according to certain immutable laws, these laws are not suddenly suspended in the liberal, socialist, or fascist soci-ety. Granted, history never occurs in a vacuum: complexities and contingencies always play a part in its seismic events. But this does not mean that we cannot discern identifiable pat-terns as to the nature of power and politics which cut across the specifics of time and place and of governmental system.

Nonetheless, we should mention at the outset the most generic complaint made by scholars who have sought to critique the thinkers I am covering in this book. James Burnham, who is one of them, dubbed these thinkers 'the Machiavellians'. This does not mean that they were all dis-ciples of Niccolò Machiavelli, but rather that they conducted their work in his spirit: to see the world *as it is and not how it ought to be.* In other words, their watchword was realism. They each had a pretence to the neutral objectivity of science. Since it is virtually impossible when dealing with a topic such as politics to eliminate the biases and preferences of the au-thor entirely, this has been fertile ground for their critics. If they could as James H. Meisel put it 'demonstrate the hidden moral bias',[8] these claims to objectivity vanish. For exam-ple, Gaetano Mosca was a kind of liberal, as was Bertrand de Jouvenel. Vilfredo Pareto was read by and influenced Beni-to Mussolini and voiced some support for fascism before he

7   John Higley, 'Elite Theory and Elites', in *Handbook of Politics: State and Society in Global Perspective*, ed. Kevin T. Leicht and J. Craig Jenkins (New York: Springer, 2010), p. 162.

8   James H. Meisel, *The Myth of the Ruling Class: Gaetano Mosca and the Elite* (Ann Arbor, MI: University of Michigan Press, 1962), p. 7.

died. Robert Michels joined the Italian fascist party after being a socialist and a syndicalist earlier in his life. Carl Schmitt joined the German National Socialist Party. James Burnham was a Trotskyist who later became a founder for the American conservative magazine, *National Review*, and was awarded the Presidential Medal of Freedom by Ronald Reagan, a Republican. Where the personal sympathies of the author leak into their otherwise 'value-free' work, it does admittedly become a potential issue. For example, C. A. Bond points out in his book *Nemesis*, some instances where de Jouvenel's otherwise exemplary work lapses into the assumptions of liberal individualism.[9] Ettore A. Albertoni shows where liberal ethical assumptions creep into the work of Mosca, especially when he posits *juridical defence* as a positive ethical category in an otherwise amoral analysis.[10] Karl Manheim criticised Vilfredo Pareto for making a 'myth' out of the idea of the man of action and said his elevation of this idea was arbitrary.[11] George Orwell complained that James Burnham too readily wrote off the prospects of making incremental and marginal increases in the standard of living for those worst off in society because of his personal antipathy to socialism.[12] All these criticisms amount to is that our authors were only human: real men living in real conditions with all the raging political debates that go on in any era. None of these criticisms significantly attack the *core* of the central arguments made by these thinkers. Thus, I have presented what is most *essential* in their various theses while stripping out what I see as the more ephemeral elements. In other words, it does not matter that Mosca favoured *juridical defence* or *separation of powers*

9   C. A. Bond, *Nemesis: The Jouvenelian vs. The Liberal Model of Human Orders* (Perth: Imperium Press, 2019), pp. 17–27.
10   Ettore A. Albertoni, *Mosca and the Theory of Elitism,* trans. Paul Goodrick (Oxford: Blackwell, 1987), pp. 51–5.
11   Karl Manheim, *Ideology and Utopia* (London: Routledge & Kegan Paul, 1936), pp. 119–30.
12   George Orwell, 'Review of The Machiavellians by James Burnham', in *Essays* (New York: Everyman's Library, 2002), p. 525.

while Pareto favoured a strong 'man of action' or Machiavellian lion. It does not matter that Samuel T. Francis called for a 'revolution of the middle' or that Carl Schmitt supported the Nazis. We must relegate all these stances to the category of *personal policy preferences*. We must separate those, which are merely contingencies owing to the circumstances and tastes of their authors, from the *essential ideas* concerning power and politics. What matters in each of their cases is whether the core principles of power and its functioning which they outlined are *true*. Does *reality* bear out in practice what they say in theory, now and always? This is the only test of a theory that aspires to realism.

The importance of taking this realist approach to power and politics is not only theoretical or academic, but also has practical implications. Those who wish to bring about political change cannot hope to do so if they adopt populist methods or have faith that at some point a critical mass of the public will suddenly reach a 'tipping point' after which elites will be inevitably toppled. Change always takes *concerted organisation* and cannot hope to be achieved simply by convincing the greatest number of people of your point of view. Power does not care, in the final analysis, how many likes you got on your Twitter account. In practice, the great bulk of people will adjust to new realities after the fact of change and reorient themselves to the new power structure one way or the other. In any case, 'manufacturing consent' can only be carried out once a group is *de facto* in power. A group may achieve *de jure* power only to find that they cannot execute or manufacture consent because they have not achieved *de facto* power—and, realistically, *de facto* power is the only power that counts.

Chapter 2
THE RULERS AND THE RULED

Gaetano Mosca's *The Ruling Class* was first published as *Elementi di scienza politica* in 1895; he then revised and massively expanded it in 1923. It was translated into English in 1939 and re-titled *The Ruling Class*; Mosca—then at the age of 80—gave his blessing to this version which was based on the second edition. I am starting with Mosca not only because this book comes first chronologically, but also because he provides us with the most basic conceptual units in our analysis of power and politics. He has two main theses in *The Ruling Class*: first, *the rulers and the ruled*; and second, *political formulas*. To these we can add two sub-theses: *the two strata of the ruling class* and *level of civilization and juridical defence*. For the remainder of this chapter let us deal with each of these in turn.

First, Mosca's central thesis, for which he is most famous, is the fact that human societies are always governed by minorities. He says:

> Among the constant facts and tendencies that are to be found in all political organisms, one is so obvious that it is apparent to the most casual eye. In all societies—from all societies that are very meagerly developed and have barely attained the dawnings of civilization, down to the most advanced and powerful societies—two classes of people appear—a class that

rules and a class that is ruled.[1]

As Mosca says, this much seems *obvious*, so why must this be pointed out and insisted upon quite so emphatically? It is because Mosca rejected any notion of popular sovereignty. Since there are always the rulers and the ruled, how can 'the people' ever be sovereign? Power does not rest *nor will ever rest* in 'the will of the people', but rather in the organised efforts of the ruling minority. People in liberal or social democracies may tell themselves otherwise, but, as Mosca contends:

> In reality the dominion of an organized minority, obeying a single impulse, over the unorganized majority is inevitable. The power of any minority is irresistible as against each single individual in the majority, who stands alone before the totality of the organized minority. A hundred men acting uniformly in concert, with a common understanding, will triumph over a thousand men who are not in accord and can therefore be dealt with one by one. Meanwhile it will be easier for the former to act in concert and have a mutual understanding simply because they are a hundred and not a thousand. It follows that the larger the political community, the smaller will the proportion of the governing minority to the governed majority be, and the more difficult will it be for the majority to organize for reaction against the minority.[2]

We might call this 'Mosca's Law': and much of his study is devoted to demonstrating this theory in practice using examples from history, and in demystifying democratic claims which try to get around this by appealing to 'the will of the people' and other such formulations. Even in the most char-

1   Gaetano Mosca, *The Ruling Class*, ed. Arthur Livingston, trans. Hannah D. Khan (1895; New York: McGraw-Hill, 1939), p. 50.
2   Mosca, *The Ruling Class*, p. 53

itable interpretation, representative democracy is simply 'elected oligarchy'.

It is worth stressing the point, as Geraint Parry does, that Mosca's thesis is more than simply saying that organised minorities always rule:

> The elitist thesis does not merely assert that in a society the minority makes the decisions and the majority obeys. This is an obvious truism with no power to explain political relationships. That fewer people issue laws, orders and instructions than receive and obey them is a fact scarcely worth commenting upon. The elitist argument is a much stronger one. It is that *the dominant minority cannot be controlled by the majority wherever democratic mechanisms are used.*[3]

Where democracies are concerned, Mosca says that 'the assumption that the elected official is the mouthpiece of the majority of his electors is as a rule not consistent with the facts':

> What happens in other forms of government—namely, that an organized minority imposes its will on the disorganized majority—happens also and to perfection, whatever the appearances to the contrary, under the representative system. When we say that the voters 'choose' their representative, we are using a language that is very inexact. The truth is that the representative *has himself elected* by the voters, and, if that phrase should seem too inflexible and too harsh to fit some cases, we might qualify it by saying that *his friends have him elected.* In elections, as in all other manifestations of social life, those who have the will and, especially, the moral, intellectual and material means to force their will upon others take the lead over the others and command them.[4]

3   Geraint Parry, *Political Elites* (London: George Allen and Unwin, 1971), p. 31, emphasis mine.
4   Mosca, *The Ruling Class*, p. 154.

Elsewhere, he points out that these 'friends' of the elected representative tend to be wealthy people who can afford to pay him to represent *their* minority interests over and above the interests of the majority. Such wealthy people also have the resources necessary to control newspapers and other media which in turn control the dissemination of information to the public and hence the formation of their individual opinions. In any case, in most cases, the alternative candidates for election will similarly have been *pre*-selected by elites, whose campaigns are managed by organised minorities, so that *any* result will favour their interests.

There are two profound consequences of Mosca's law. First, because it is a permanent aspect of human society, the classical liberal notion that there is an antagonism between the state and society is rendered as utopian nonsense:

> From our point of view there can be no antagonism between state and society. The state is to be looked upon merely as that part of society which performs the political function. Considered in this light, all questions touching interference or noninterference by the state come to assume a new aspect. Instead of asking what the limits of state activity ought to be, we try to find out what the best type of political organization is, which type, in other words, enables all the elements that have a political significance in a given society to be best utilized and specialized, best subjected to reciprocal control and to the principle of individual responsibility for the things that are done in the respective domains.[5]

Mosca's ultimate answer to this is a kind of Machiavellian mixed-Republic in which there are competing power centres and in which different social types are part of the process of power. Senators, for example, should not be elected but rather men of distinction and social standing in other fields who serve as a duty and without a wage. In this

5   Mosca, *The Ruling Class*, pp. 158–9.

respect, his vision of a balanced system is not that far re-moved from the original vision of the American Founding Fathers. With that said, he is highly sceptical and critical of written constitutions, and prefers as his model the more organic British system in which the wisdom of the ruling class has facilitated change without violent revolution. However, Mosca's positive prescriptions are less import-ant than his clear-eyed diagnosis of reality. Which brings us to the second consequence of Mosca's Law: he is highly critical of Herbert Spencer's notion that there is any real distinction between military states founded on force and coercion and liberal states founded on voluntary associa-tion and trade. He argues:

> Any political organization is both voluntary and co-ercive at one and the same time—voluntary because it arises from the very nature of man, as was long ago noted by Aristotle, and coercive because it is a neces-sary fact, the human being finding himself unable to live otherwise. It is natural, therefore, and at the same time indispensable, that where there are men there should automatically be a society, and that when there is a society there should also be a state—that is to say, a minority that rules and a majority that is ruled by the ruling minority.[6]

Thus, we must bear in mind that when Mosca is described as a 'liberal', it is not in the sense of being a small-state classical liberal or what is today called a libertarian. He was liberal only in the sense that he opposed absolutism and generally supported separation of powers and their distribution across social types. We will return to this theme when we consider Carl Schmitt and Bertrand de Jouvenel who independently came to understand that separation of powers is a myth sel-dom, if ever, realised in practice.

Now we must ask a question: why do the majority assent

6   Mosca, *The Ruling Class*, p. 96.

to the rule of the minority? According to Mosca it is because they, at least tacitly, subscribe to the 'political formula' of the ruling class. The political formula, or 'principle of sovereignty', is defined as the 'legal and moral basis, or principle, on which the power of the political class rests'.[7] The two chief examples Mosca provides are those political formulas that are based on supernatural beliefs, for example, the Divine Right of kings, and those based on the notion of popular sovereignty or 'the will of the people'. However, these myths are not necessarily to be taken as cynical lies told by the rulers to hoodwink the masses but are necessary for the smooth operation of the whole society. Georges Sorel called them 'myths', Karl Manheim, and later the Marxist, Louis Althusser, called them 'ideologies'.[8] Indeed, Mosca recognises that a 'moral unity' between the rulers and the ruled can create almost miraculous situations in which they may overcome materially stronger external powers in war. Today we might think of the Vietnamese against the Americans, or the Afghani Taliban against the Americans. Mosca's examples include the Spanish against the French in 1808 and various so-called barbarian groups, such as the Franks, against the Romans at the fall of their empire.[9] However, it is not enough for the ruled majority alone to have this moral unity, they could show great courage but will still likely fail if they are not met by an equal moral unity in the ruling class. Mosca gives the example of the kingdom of Naples against the French in 1798–9 where the people were united, but they were betrayed by the pro-French sympathies of their ruling class: 'Treason, therefore and, more than treason, the unending suspicion of treason, paralysed all resistance, disorganized the regular army [...]

7   Mosca, *The Ruling Class*, p. 70.
8   Georges Sorel, *Reflections on Violence*, trans. T. E. Hulme, ed. Jeremy Jennings (1908; Imperium Press, 2022); Karl Manheim, *Ideology and Utopia* (London: Routledge & Kegan Paul, 1936); Louis Althusser, *Lenin and Philosophy and Other Essays*, trans. Ben Brewster (1971; New York: Monthly Review Press, 2001).
9   Mosca, *The Ruling Class*, p. 109.

and diminished the effectiveness of a spontaneous popular resistance […] which might have triumphed.'[10] The inverse is also true: a ruling class who show moral unity will likely fail if the ruled do not share their convictions; again, we might think of American foreign escapades since World War II.

No ruling class can survive without an effective political formula. 'Ruling classes may fail to adapt their formula to the changed demands of society; or ruling classes may renew themselves or be renewed. In the first case, failure to renew the formula may signal the end of the ruling class; in the second case, the formula might be retained (the British crown would be a good example).'[11] A new ruling class can arise out of the 'people' with a new political formula: 'the ruled mass remain the hummus out of which grow leading groups.'[12] But if this is the case—and if a political formula can be so powerful as an animating spirit as to be in Mosca's own terms 'quasi-miraculous'[13]—then why is he so adamant that the political formula of popular sovereignty should be demystified and debunked as factually fraudulent? First, remember that Mosca's goal was not to instruct rulers in the *art* of politics, but rather to outline a *science* of politics which sees things in the cold light of day. Second, Mosca saw the political formula of the French Revolution—liberty, equality and fraternity—as being entirely destructive because it is impossible to put into practice.[14] The democratic principle is simply one wrong-headed offshoot of this. Mosca points out that 'the will of the people' and the notion of Divine Right are both, in practice, taken on faith and are beyond reason. But 'the will of the people', unlike Divine Right, is the product of enlight-

10   Mosca, *The Ruling Class*, p. 110.
11   James H. Meisel, *The Myth of the Ruling Class: Gaetano Mosca and the Elite* (Ann Arbor, MI: University of Michigan Press, 1962), p. 17.
12   Mosca, *The Ruling Class*, 17.
13   Mosca, *The Ruling Class*, p. 109.
14   Ettore A. Albertoni, *Mosca and the Theory of Elitism*, trans. Paul Goodrick (Oxford: Blackwell, 1987), p. 26.

enment rationalism and is *demonstrably false.* This falsity has practical and often violent consequences which supernatural beliefs do not. 'Mosca argued that democracy was inherently bad, and that the desire to rectify these problems via reforms aimed at instituting "true democracy" were totally misconceived. They would only make matters worse.'[15] The cold reality that 'the people' *are not and can never be* sovereign will continually rear its head, so it is quite ineffective as a source of moral unity. In other words, it acts as a constant source of class resentment so that the unity of ruler and ruled, which can be so powerful, never fully comes about.

Mosca 'rejected any monistic view of history—that is a theory of history which holds that there is one single cause that accounts for everything that happens in society.'[16] The political formula is important but it is not the *sole* driver in history. Hence, Mosca's theory of regime change—the replacement of one ruling class with another—is quite dynamic. He states:

> As soon as there is a shift in the balance of political forces [...] then the manner in which the ruling class is constituted changes also. If a new source of wealth develops in a society, if a practical importance of knowledge grows, if an old religion declines or a new one is born, if a new current of ideas spreads, then, simultaneously, far-reaching dislocations occur in the ruling class.[17]

This contrasts with Karl Marx for whom the sole driver of history is always economic and in contrast with Pareto, who—as we shall see in the next chapter—put the circulation of elites down to psychology.[18] Mosca's conception may seem

15   Richard Bellamy, *Modern Italian Social Theory* (Oxford: Blackwell, 1987), p. 41.
16   James Burnham, *The Machiavellians: Defenders of Freedom* (London: Putnam, 1943), p. 61.
17   Mosca, *The Ruling Class*, p. 65.
18   Robert D. Putnam, *The Comparative Study of Political Elites* (Englewood Cliffs, NJ: Prentice-Hall, 1976), pp. 168-9.

less neat in comparison, but as a student of history, he knew that history is often messy, and complex, and does not fit easily into any abstract scheme. He rejected 'the single-factor fallacy.'[19] For him, the prime movers in history were disturbances to 'social forces', which can be brought about through changes in economic conditions or technology or brought about by new ideas. By 'social forces', H. Stuart Hughes explains, 'he meant the major public interests constituted by businessmen and agriculturalists, intellectuals and the military'.[20] The ruling class must adapt to the new conditions or else they will be replaced with a new one more apt to rule in the new circumstances.

Let us move on to the third important idea in Mosca: the idea that the ruling class has two distinct strata. No man rules alone, as they say, and any governing body is going to need an apparatus of people who fulfil the day-to-day functions of running the place, as well as an arguably even more important function: that of propagating the political formula. The first strata of the ruling class are simply those people who hold the positions of high office. It could be the King and his court of high-ranking nobles or the Prime Minister, his cabinet and his party, but we can visibly see who is 'in charge'. This is the highest stratum of the ruling class, but as Mosca outlines late in the second edition of *The Ruling Class*, in chapter XV:

> Below the highest stratum in the ruling class there is always, even in autocratic systems, another that is much more numerous and comprises all the capacities for leadership in the country. Without such a class any sort of social organization would be impossible. The higher stratum would not in itself be sufficient or leading and directing the activities of the

19   Franco Ferrarotti, 'The Italian Context: Pareto and Mosca', in *Pareto and Mosca*, ed. James H. Meisel (Englewood Cliffs, NJ: Prentice-Hall, 1965), p. 132.
20   H. Stuart Hughes, *Consciousness and Society* (Brighton: The Harvester Press, 1979), p. 256.

masses. In the last analysis, therefore, the stability of
any political organism depends on the level of morality, intelligence and activity that this second stratum
has attained [...] Any intellectual or moral deficien-
cies in this second stratum, accordingly, represent a
graver danger to the political structure, and one that
is harder to repair, than the presence of similar de-
ficiencies in the few dozen persons who control the
workings of the state machine.[21]

We should note that Vilfredo Pareto also has these two categories which he calls 'the governing elite' and the 'non-governing elite'.[22] Pareto's *Treatise* was published in 1916. This
section from Mosca comes in the second part of the *Elementi*,
which was added in 1923. Mosca acknowledges Pareto briefly in the introduction to this second part, which is significant as the two men were known not to get on.[23] He also
acknowledged him again in the final chapter of his *History of
Modern Political Doctrines* published in 1933.[24] This distinction
between the two strata of the ruling class is one of the few
places where we can trace the direct influence of Pareto on
Mosca's thinking.

The Italian Marxist theorist, Antonio Gramsci, was un-
happy with the apparent vagueness in defining the ruling
class this broadly, since the non-governing elite appears to
encompass a broad section of society, if not the entire middle class. He declared that 'Mosca's "political class" is noth-

21   Mosca, *The Ruling Class*, pp. 403–4.
22   Vilfredo Pareto, *Compendium of General Sociology*, ed. Elisabeth Abbott (1916; Minneapolis, MN: University of Minnesota
Press, 1980), p. 274.
23   See Mosca, *The Ruling Class*, p. 331.
24   This chapter is reprinted in *Meisel, The Myth of the Ruling
Class*, pp. 382–91. This is one of the few books of Mosca's, other than *The Ruling Class*, to be translated into English; it was published: A Short History of Political Philosophy, trans. by Sondra Z.
Koff (1933; New York: Thomas Cromwell, 1972), the chapter is
pp. 247-57.

ing but the intellectual section of the ruling group.'[25] Here, we must be careful. It seems to me that Mosca has in mind, principally, civil servants, bureaucrats, and other people responsible for the day-to-day management of the state. To use James Burnham's later phrase, he is thinking of the *managerial class*. Gramsci seems to have in mind the intelligentsia, those people responsible for disseminating and controlling the flow of information and ideas, opinion shapers, myth-makers, ideologists, upholders and justifiers of the political formula, or, if you prefer, a *priest class*. While this is certainly implied in the emphasis Mosca gives to the political formula, he does not explicitly stress these ideological functions of the non-governing elite, which were central to Gramsci's work. In fact, Gramsci's 'own theory of intellectuals is supposed to represent an improvement on Mosca's theory of the political class.'[26] Mosca, rather, stresses the practical considerations and deals with churches and religions in a separate chapter, and seemingly in isolation.[27] He argues that at certain times, ideologies can be 'mere pretexts' to justify conflict. However, he acknowledges that universal religions such as Christianity or Islam can constitute 'a very close bond between most disparate peoples who differ widely in race and language'. But by the same token, 'also act as estranging forces of great potency between populations that cherish different beliefs.'[28] Thus religious sentiments, in Mosca's view, can either be skin-deep and post-hoc rationalised or deeply held and either a force for uniting disparate people or sowing division within an otherwise homogenous group. Such doctrines may or may not be utilised as part of a political formula, but it seems that Mosca sees religions functioning somewhat independently of

25   Quoted in Tom Bottomore, *Elites and Society*, 2nd edition (1964; New York and London: Routledge, 1993), p. 5.

26   Maurice A. Finocchiaro, *Beyond Right and Left: Democratic Elitism in Mosca and Gramsci* (New Haven, MA: Yale University Press, 1999), p. 90.

27   See Mosca, *The Ruling Class*, pp. 163–98.

28   Mosca, *The Ruling Class*, pp. 164, 75, 76.

the ruling class. And he gives special treatment to priests *as a ruling class* in theocratic states.[29] I think it would be fair to say that the role of official state ideologue, which is to say, the people responsible for propagating the political formula and ensuring it is believed by the masses, is somewhat underdeveloped in Mosca. Marxists such as Antonio Gramsci and Louis Althusser took this a lot further, and the so-called 'long march through the institutions' of the Left is largely a testament to their thinking. In the canon of elite theory, the understanding of the role of intellectuals in the ruling class is greatly expanded by James Burnham and his protégé Samuel T. Francis, whom we will consider in later chapters.

A fourth distinctive feature of Mosca's analysis is his concept of 'level of civilisation'. In his introduction to the English version of *The Ruling Class*, Arthur Livingstone provides a description of what Mosca means by this:

> It is a criterion that is definable to a high grade of approximation as multiplicity of activities; grade or quality of achievement in each; size and stability of social cohesion and, therefore, offensive and defensive power; standard of living and distribution of wealth; control of nature and utilization of that control; and so on—so on even to the 'higher things' themselves.[30]

In material economic terms, we might say that when Mosca talks about a 'high level' of civilization he is describing a very complex society with advanced division of labour which affords both material prosperity and technological progress. However, as societies advance to higher levels, a robust bureaucracy becomes a raw practical necessity, simply to manage the administration of so many people. Thus, Mosca identifies two key forms of social system: feudal and bureaucratic. In a feudal state there are no separation of powers: 'the economic, the judicial, the administrative, the military' functions

29   Mosca, *The Ruling Class*, pp. 59, 92, 343.
30   Arthur Livingstone, 'Introduction', in *Mosca, The Ruling Class*, p. xxxi.

of the ruling class are 'exercised simultaneously by the same individuals.'[31] These powers are vested in a local lord in a decentralised system of hierarchical patronage headed by a king. This has the advantage of a high level of social cohesion at the local level. Mosca points out that lords and their vassals were close in sentiment and manners: 'The baron knew his vassals personally. He thought and felt as they did. He had the same superstitions, the same habits, the same language. [...] he was a man whom they understood perfectly [...] with whom they sometimes got drunk.'[32] However, feudal states are inefficient at quickly mobilising men for military campaigns and are subject to internal quarrels between rival lords. In contrast, the bureaucratic state, which has succeeded in centralising taxation, has greater specialization of the key functions of government and can maintain a standing army. Mosca says: 'The greater the number of officials who perform public duties and receive their salaries from the central government or from its local agencies, the more bureaucratic the state.'[33] The key marker of a bureaucratic state is not the fact of centralisation—since many of these functions could be performed by private enterprise—but rather that they are performed by salaried employees and separated out into specialisms. In this respect, 1930s USA, the UK of the same era, Nazi Germany, Fascist Italy, the USSR, were all equally bureaucratic states.

However, in Mosca's estimation, a further ethical criterion must be considered when judging the 'level of civilization': juridical defence. He explains:

> [I]n a highly developed civilization not only do moral instincts—and for that matter selfish passions—become more refined, more conscious, more perfect. In a society in which political organization has made great progress, moral discipline is itself unquestionably greater, and the too selfish acts that are inhibited, or obstructed, by the reciprocal surveillance and

31 Mosca, *The Ruling Class*, p. 81.
32 Mosca, *The Ruling Class*, p. 112.
33 Mosca, *The Ruling Class.*, p. 83.

> restraint of the individuals who compose the society
> are more numerous and more clearly defined.[34]

This is somewhat different from saying that the more bureaucratic a society becomes, the higher its level, since one might easily imagine a bureaucratic state that has poor juridical defence. Mosca has in mind an independent and fair judiciary backed by strong rule of law which will, in turn, help to maintain a morally upstanding and law-abiding citizenry. If the ruling class keep political prisoners and act in an arbitrary manner, do not give the ruled the right to a fair trial, do not persecute serious crimes and let criminals loose on the streets, and so on, then it is evidence of a lack of juridical defence. Samuel T. Francis coined the phrase 'anarcho-tyranny' in 2004 to describe the situation in which a highly bureaucratic and modern system such as the USA or the UK today could fail in meeting the basic standards of juridical defence.[35] Juridical defence could only be maintained, according to Mosca, if there were independent competing power centres in society that were kept from converging—in effect, inter-elite competition would keep the central institutions more 'honest', which is easier said than done as we shall see when we come to consider later thinkers.

Mosca's *The Ruling Class* is a book with many fascinating insights and nuggets of political wisdom from its author as he navigates his way through many moments in history. He is almost 'impressionistic [...] what he lost in logical rigour was amply compensated for by the flexibility and richness of his analysis of political life.'[36] For us today it is an invaluable guide for two chief reasons: first, it punctures absolutely what I would like to call the *populist delusion* that if conditions get bad enough, if the plebians become too disgruntled

---

34   Mosca, *The Ruling Class*, p. 125.
35   Samuel T. Francis, 'Anarcho-Tyranny – Where Multiculturalism Leads', VDare (December 12, 2004): https://vdare.com/articles/anarcho-tyranny-where-multiculturalism-leads.
36   Bellamy, *Modern Italian Social Theory*, p. 35.

with their leaders, then the people will rise up and overthrow them. This, as Mosca shows, has never happened in history, not even once. This brings us to the second key practical use of his work: that if people want change even at a time of popular and widespread resentment of the ruling class, they can only hope to achieve that change by becoming a tightly knit and organised minority themselves and, in effect, displacing the old ruling class. This, of course, is no easy process and Mosca was not in the business of outlining what needed to be done: he was the detached political scientist, not Vladimir Lenin. He is also vague as to the precise mechanisms that might lead to the replacement of one ruling class with another. How can a new ruling class propagate a political formula more apt to the circumstances than the old one, for example? Mosca's analysis is pitched at a panoramic level of remove, and so the business of political *change* seems almost automatic. It will be up to some of the other thinkers whom I will be considering in this book to fill in some of these gaps.

Chapter 3
THE CIRCULATION OF ELITES

Vilfredo Pareto published his mammoth four-volume *Treatise of on General Sociology* in 1916. It was translated into English and published as *The Mind and Society* in 1935 by the same editor, Arthur Livingstone, who brought out Mosca's *The Ruling Class* four years later. Given the sheer size of this text—which runs to over 2,000 pages and 2 million words—I have relied on the abridged version the *Compendium of General Sociology*, which Pareto approved. This version still runs to over 450 pages. It was published in Italian in 1920 and finally received an English version in 1980.[1] However, for the sake of convenience and consistency, I have referenced the full version of *The Mind and Society* throughout because it is customary to refer to Pareto's numbered paragraphs, and these differ in the *Compendium*. Unlike Mosca, who rooted his analysis in history, Pareto devised an entire system of sociology driven by his recognition of the limitations of economics. His goal was to 'describe what society is like, and to discover some general laws in terms of which society operates' without 'expressing any ideal of what society and government ought to be.'[2] This marks a second contrast to Mosca, whose analysis, as we saw in the last chapter, contained positive and morally norma-

1   Vilfredo Pareto, *Compendium of General Sociology*, ed. Elisabeth Abbott (Minneapolis, MN: University of Minnesota Press, 1980).
2   James Burnham, *The Machiavellians: Defenders of Freedom* (London: Putnam, 1943), p. 124.

tive elements such as the notion of juridical defence; Pareto's analysis is wholly cast in the neutral and amoral mode of 'scientific analysis'. For our purposes, we are interested in his famous concept of 'The Circulation of Elites', but in order to understand this, it is necessary at least to have some knowledge of his entire sociological system. I will first outline Pareto's concepts of sentiments, residues, and derivations before turning to his notion of the circulation of the elites.

Pareto argued that most human action is 'non-logical', that is, not animated by conscious beliefs but rather by instincts which he called 'sentiments' manifested as 'residues'. In his introduction to the *Compendium*, Joseph Lopreato provides a good summary of what this means:

> [I]nstead of saying that belief B is the cause of action A, it may be more informative, more theoretically fundamental, to hypothesize that both A and B are rooted in the third factor, X. The theory of residues is the result of Pareto's search for the human X.[3]

'Sentiments', then, are the ultimate determinant of human thought and action (X), they manifest in the real world as observable 'residues' (A), but since humans also feel a need for logic, they post-hoc rationalise these residues by generating arguments (B) which Pareto called 'derivations'. Pareto's thinking bears some resemblance to Adam Smith's *Theory of Sentiments* and David Hume's famous maxim that 'Reason is, and ought only to be the slave of the passions'.[4] This insight has since been underlined by studies in modern psychology such as Daniel Kahneman's *Thinking Fast and Slow* or Jonathan Haidt's *The Righteous Mind*.[5] Intuition comes first; rea-

3   Joseph Lopreato, 'Introduction', in Burnham, *The Machiavellians*, p. xxviii.
4   Adam Smith, *The Theory of Moral Sentiments*, ed. Ryan Patrick Henley (1759; New York and London: Penguin, 2010); David Hume, A Treatise of Human Nature (1739; New York: Dover Publications, 2003), p. 295.
5   See Daniel Kahneman, *Thinking Fast and Slow* (New York

soning follows as a *justification* for what one has already felt at a 'gut level'. At a societal level these justifications manifest as ideologies, theologies, doctrines of all sorts, and these specific manifestations are 'derivations'. However, the root of any given derivation will be a more general 'residue' which in turn has been generated by a 'sentiment'. Humans seem to have a deeply felt need for a sense of purification, which is the sentiment, thus they have the have the general *idea* of purification, which is the residue, but any specific manifestation of this—such as the Christian ritual of baptism, for example— is a derivation.

Pareto lists over 40 residues which correspond to about 20 sentiments. He then groups these residues into six classes. This classification takes up the entirety of volume two of the full *Treatise* which is mostly cut out of the *Compendium*. Most accounts only consider the first two, but in the interests of providing a glimpse of the fuller picture, let us list all six of them:

Class I: Instinct for Combinations

Class II: Persistence of Aggregates

Class III: Need for Expressing Sentiments by External Acts

Class IV: Residues Connected with Sociality

Class V: Integrity of the Individual and His Appurtenances

and London: Penguin, 2011) and Jonathan Haidt, *The Righteous Mind: Why Good People Are Divided by Religion and Politics* (New York: Random House, 2012). I considered these works at length in Neema Parvini, *Shakespeare and Cognition: Thinking Fast and Slow through Character* (New York and London: Palgrave Macmillan, 2015) and *Shakespeare's Moral Compass* (Edinburgh: Edinburgh University Press, 2018), and, in a more distilled form in *The Defenders of Liberty: Human Nature, Individualism, and Property Rights* (New York and London: Palgrave Macmillan, 2020), pp. 9–14.

Class VI: The Sex Residue.[6]

None of these classes are mutually exclusive and all people will possess the residues they comprise but in varying degrees of strength. Under each class, Pareto lists specific residues. Since Classes I and II are the only ones relevant to his analysis of the elites, a summary of them by Lopreato will suffice:

> The combinations [Class I] are responsible for bringing about new ideas, new cognitive and moral systems, new technologies, new social and cultural forms, and so forth. They are, in short, the endogenous factors of sociocultural evolution. [...] [T]he persistences [Class II] are the judges in the final instance of what shall be programmed into the social order. They may be viewed as the basic selective mechanisms in socio-cultural evolution [...] [P]eople strong in persistences [Class II] tend to be patriotic, tradition-loving, religious, familistic, frugal in their economic habits, inclined toward the use of force and confrontation in political matters, adept at deferring gratification. Conversely, persons strong in combinations [Class I] are culture-relativists; they value change as an end itself; they are hedonistic, rationalistic, individualistic, dedicated to spending and entrepreneurship; they are also inclined toward ruse, deception, and diplomacy in political matters.[7]

These two forces, which we might easily recognise today as liberal and conservative, combine to create a 'social equilibrium'. If Class II predominates, the rate of innovation and change slows; if Class I predominates it speeds up. However, I would exercise caution in using Class I and Class II as prox-

6   Vilfredo Pareto, *The Mind and Society*, ed. Arthur Livingstone, trans. Andrew Bongiorno and Arthur Livingstone, 4 vols (1916; New York: Harcourt, Brace and Company, 1935), vol 2, §888, pp. 516–19.
7   Lopreato, 'Introduction', pp. xxxii–xxxiii.

ies for 'liberal' and 'conservative' or 'left' and 'right' because in any given society the Class II types could be maintaining the persistence of liberal values, or indeed, the Class I types could be agitating for a radical change towards conservative values. A man like Joseph Stalin—one of the most famous communists in history—identifiably had stronger Class II tendencies.

Nonetheless, given the dynamic of the relationship between Classes I and II, we might recognise over time a certain ratcheting effect whereby Class II continually institute the ideas of Class I, 'programming them into the social order', such that history would trend in a Class I direction. This may well have been what Curtis Yarvin had in mind when he said that 'Cthulhu may swim slowly. But he always swims left'.[8] However, again, I should caution against seeing Class I and II in terms of left and right since in a given set of circumstances Class I tendencies could pull in a right-wing direction; in any case, the terms 'left' and 'right' are rendered somewhat meaningless by elite theory. Besides, Pareto rejected the idea that history had a direction or shape as such. He was 'extremely critical of cyclical theories (e.g. Plato's and Vico's) and argued 'that history does not repeat itself' but rather 'there are certain underlying forces (the residues[...]) that are constantly at work in wave-like fashion.'[9] At the same time, he maintained that there were 'no *linear* rules of social evolution; instead, one encounters ceaseless fluctuations, an eternal return of periodic oscillations.'[10] He also rejected any theory of *progress*:

> Once experience is admitted (it matters little how)

8   Mencius Moldbug, 'A Gentle Introduction to Unqualified Reservations' (Unqualified Reservations: 2015): https://www.unqualified-reservations.org/2009/01/gentle-introduction-to-unqualified/.
9   Lopreato, 'Introduction', p. xxiv.
10   Alain de Benoist, *The View from the Right*, 3 vols (1977; London: Arktos, 2018), vol 2, p. 143.

within the theological edifice, the latter begins to crumble—such portion of it, of course, as stands within the experimental domain, for the other wings are safe from any attack by experience. [...] So years, centuries, go by; peoples, governments, manners and systems of living, pass away; and all along new theologies, new systems of metaphysics, keep replacing the old, and each new one is reputed more 'true' or much 'better' than its predecessors. And in certain cases they may really be better, if by 'better' we mean more helpful to society; but more 'true', no, if by the term we mean accord with experimental reality. One faith cannot be more scientific than another, and experimental reality is equally overreached by polytheism, Islamism, and Christianity (whether Catholic, Protestant, Liberal, Modernist, or of any other variety); by the innumerable metaphysical sects, including the Kantian, the Hegelian, the Bergsonian, and not excluding the positivistic sects of Comte, Spencer, and other eminent writers too numerous to mention; by the faiths of solidaristes, humanitarians, anti-clericals, and worshippers of Progress; and by as many other faiths as have existed, exist, or can be imagined.[11]

Unlike Mosca, who admitted that historical change was driven by some combination of material changes, technological changes, and the influence of new ideas, Pareto's system reduces such changes to second-order effects of the primary real cause of change: residues driven by underlying instinctual sentiments. Historical change has no direction or purpose, it does not repeat, it has no shape, it simply convulses in response to these deeply-felt 'non-logical' human needs.

Pareto then categorises derivations into four main classes:

Class I: Assertion, simply maxims constantly re-

11   Pareto, *The Mind and Society*, vol 1, §616, pp. 371–2.

peated to become accepted truths.

Class II: Authority, whether an individual, a group of individuals, a deity, or tradition.

Class III: Accords with Sentiment or Principles, sentiments converted into abstractions and declarations of universal laws, very similar to Mosca's 'political formulas'.

Class IV: Verbal Proofs, logical sophistry designed to affirm sentiments with which the speaker and listener already agree.[12]

His analysis of these four classes of derivations takes up most of volume three of *The Mind and Society*. Pareto takes his value-free analysis to a logical extreme point in this section and essentially concludes that all moral philosophies in human history have been a form of delusion designed to justify the more instinctual residues. We have already glimpsed in his rejection of theories of history, an almost nihilistic tendency in Pareto to dismiss all *ideas* as being meaningless second-order effects which have no other effect than to justify what humans already feel. This is a radically sceptical position that many people will instinctually seek to reject. But Pareto would predict this reaction because humans have a deeply-felt sentiment to believe in 'certain theories that are experimentally false' but which nonetheless have a 'social utility'.

> So great is the need of such things which human beings feel that if one structure happens to collapse, another is straightway reared of the same material. [...] [S]ince society cannot do without the thing A, some of the defenders of the old faith P will merely replace it with a new faith Q, no less discordant with experience.[13]

---

12   Pareto, *The Mind and Society*, vol 3, §1419, p. 899.
13   Pareto, *The Mind and Society*, vol 1, §616, pp. 371–2.

'Truth value and social utility do not necessarily coincide.'[14] Since most of us have some positive believe in a faith, doctrine, or 'political formula' to use Mosca's phrase, we will not wish to admit that what we believe are simply delusions or 'beautiful lies'. One thing surely no one can deny, however, is that in the absence of an old faith, the void *will be filled* by new ones. Recent experience has shown us that Christianity gave way to rationalism which gave way to positivism and finally to scientism; feudalism gave way to liberalism which gave way to socialism and notions of 'social justice'; Divine Right gave way to parliamentarism and democracy, and so on. 'In Pareto's eyes, there is no difference at all between belief in a classless society and the belief in angels and devils; the end purpose is different, but not the nature of the belief, nor the method of argumentation.'[15] All that the various arguments and justifications—for what are always, in the final analysis, non-logical faiths—show is that human beings have 'an *inclination towards rationality*, not the fact of *being rational.*'[16] Pareto maintains that while this is objectively *true*, humans will never admit it of themselves. One might object that knowledge of this fact has *no use* in terms of making society better for us, but let us recall that Pareto—again, unlike Mosca—did not wish to give any positive prescriptions on what *ought* to be whatsoever; the true Machiavellian considers only what *is*. His project amounts to saying, 'you may not like it, but this is what human beings are when stripped of all ideological baggage: do with that knowledge what you will.'

However, this opens the door to the most common criticism of Pareto by scholars of all stripes, namely, how can he escape his own system? H. Stuart Hughes accuses him

14   Joseph V. Femia, *Against the Masses: Varieties of Anti-Democratic Thought since the French Revolution* (Oxford: Oxford University Press, 2001), p. 70.
15   Julien Freund, quoted in de Benoist, *The View from the Right*, vol 2, p. 146.
16   Benoist, *The View from the Right*, vol 2, p. 146.

of a 'certain arbitrariness'.[17] Tom Bottomore says he makes no attempt to show the residues, on which he places so much emphasis, 'actually exist'.[18] Geraint Parry argues that 'Pareto offers no satisfactory reasons for accepting his view that "residues", as the constants, are more significant historically than the ideologies they give rise to'.[19] Richard Bellamy contends that 'far from providing a "neutral" description of human behaviour, Pareto merely endowed his own ideological leanings with a spurious scientific status.'[20] These criticisms cannot go unaddressed here. First, the methodological objections are valid, but as I have already noted, studies in modern psychology have provided much empirical evidence for Pareto's claims; many behavioural and evolutionary scholars have accepted the view that 'intuition comes first, and reasoning follows.'[21] Second, the wider point that Pareto's work is in some sense the product of his *own* 'residues' is often predicated on the fact that Pareto died having apparent sympathies for fascism and justified his preference for the use of force or violence.[22] The extent of Pareto's actual support for fascism is widely disputed,[23] it seems to me partly a product of motivated Mosca scholars who sought to make a comparison which cast Pareto in an unfavourable light.[24] Such debates are

17   H. Stuart Hughes, *Consciousness and Society* (Brighton: The Harvester Press, 1979), p. 264.
18   Tom Bottomore, *Elites and Society*, 2nd edn (1964; New York and London: Routledge, 1993), p. 38.
19   Geraint Parry, *Political Elites* (London: George Allen and Unwin, 1971), p. 49.
20   Richard Bellamy, *Modern Italian Social Theory* (Oxford: Blackwell, 1987), p. 27.
21   Kahneman, *Thinking Fast and Slow*; Haidt, *The Righteous Mind*.
22   This is the thrust of the account in Bellamy, *Modern Italian Social Theory*.
23   See Lopreato, 'Introduction', pp. xviii–xx.
24   See, for example, James H. Meisel, *The Myth of the Ruling Class: Gaetano Mosca and the Elite* (Ann Arbor, MI: University of Michigan

quite beyond my scope here, but the idea that Pareto's justification of human violence was somehow morally nor-
mative and a preference rather than a simple statement of
a constant fact of history relies itself on a morally norma-
tive view that peace is the norm and constant from which
violence diverges, and must be justified. Surely, the fact
that humans are prone to the use of force and violence is
non-controversial? Third, there is the more penetrating
critique that his argument is self-refuting: namely that his
whole edifice is simply what he 'already feels'. This would
not refute the correctness or validity of Pareto's project
since *if the theory of the sentiments and residues is true* then
the fruits of Pareto's own instinctual feelings simply tell us
profound truths about human nature itself, in the manner
that one might expect of, say, a William Shakespeare.[25] In
other words, that the ideas may have their root in some
non-logical aspect of Pareto's thinking and feeling is not
significant. Pareto does not say that all derivations based
on residues and sentiments are delusional, he says it is delusional to believe that there might be derivations that are
somehow *not* rooted in residues and sentiments. Since almost all other derivations (i.e. all those other than his) do
not acknowledge this fact, they are therefore delusional.
However, even with these caveats, I am not sure that Pareto can escape the charge that his absolute adherence to
this view itself amounts to a faith position.

Now that we have some idea of the core of Pareto's
thinking, let us come back to the circulation of elites.
Recall the Class I and II residues outlined above. Pareto
maintained that changes in history were chiefly down to
alternations within the proportions of Class I and Class II

Press, 1962), p. 9.
25   For a book-length project treating Shakespeare in exactly
this manner see Neema Parvini, *Shakespeare's Moral Compass* (Edinburgh: Edinburgh University Press, 2018).

residues among the elites. In one of his most famous and most quoted phrases, 'History is a graveyard of aristocracies.'[26] Class I residues correspond to Machiavelli's 'foxes', while Class II residues correspond to Machiavelli's 'lions'. Foxes are adept at manipulation and manufacturing consent, 'specialists on persuasion', while lions are adept at the use of force, 'specialists on coercion'.[27] Although he does not refer to them specifically, Pareto seems to take for granted Mosca's arguments that the rulers, the ruled, and minority organisation always and everywhere overcome the disorganised masses. He also maintains the distinction between the higher and lower strata of the ruling class, which he calls 'governing elite' and 'non-governing elite'.[28] Still, however, it is the underlying residues that drive change, while arguments generated by elites are ephemera, post-hoc rationalisations, that do not affect the outcome of anything:

> In politics all ruling classes have at all times identified their own interests with the 'interests of the country.' When politicians are afraid of a too rapid increase in the number of proletarians, they are for birth-control and show that Malthusianism is to the interests of public and country. If, instead, they are afraid a population may prove inadequate for their designs, they are against birth-control, and show just as conclusively that their interest is the interest of public and country. And all that is accepted as long as residues remain favourable. The situation changes as residues change never in view of arguments pro or contra.[29]

'The character of society, Pareto holds, is above all the charac-

26   Pareto, *The Mind and Society*, vol 3, §2053, p. 1430.
27   Harold D. Lasswell and C. Easton Rothwell, *The Comparative Study of Elites* (Stanford, CA: Stanford University Press, 1952), p. 16.
28   Pareto, *The Mind and Society*, vol 3, §2032, p. 1423.
29   Pareto, *The Mind and Society*, vol 4, §1499, p. 949.

ter of its elite; its accomplishments are the accomplishments of its elites; its history is properly understood as the history of its elite; successful predictions about the future are based upon evidence drawn from the study of the composition and structure of its elite.'[30] At any given time, the composition of elites will shift more towards foxes or to lions. 'The cunning foxes retain power for some time by their cleverness in forming and reforming coalitions, but "force is also essential in the exercise of government". Eventually the more forceful counter-elite of lions, willing to use coercion and violence, capture power from the fainthearted foxes and impose order and discipline. In time, however, the intellectual incompetence and inflexibility of the lions lead to their gradual decline and infiltration by the more imaginative foxes.'[31] While both Class I and Class II residues predominate among elites, the non-elite, which is to say the ruled, are always overwhelmingly of the Class II type.[32] Thus if Class I dominates for too long, and especially if they have become enraptured with doctrines of universal humanitarianism, a counter-elite will form from the non-elite 'one way or the other' which includes violent revolution.[33]

Let us dwell briefly on this final point; Pareto returns to it himself later in *The Mind and Society*. In what follows, when Pareto says 'the subject class', he means the ruled majority:

> As regards the subject class, we get the following relations [...]: 1. When the subject class contains a number of individuals disposed to use force and with capable leaders to guide them, the governing class is, in many cases, overthrown and another takes its place. That is easily the case where governing classes are inspired by humanitarian sentiments primarily,

30 Burnham, *The Machiavellians*, p. 154.
31 Robert D. Putnam, *The Comparative Study of Political Elites* (Englewood Cliffs, NJ: Prentice-Hall, 1976), p. 167.
32 Pareto, *The Mind and Society*, vol 3, §1811, p. 1260.
33 Burnham, *The Machiavellians*, p. 159.

and very easily if they do not find ways to assimilate the exceptional individuals who come to the front in the subject classes. A humanitarian aristocracy that is closed or stiffly exclusive represents the maximum of insecurity. 2. It is far more difficult to overthrow a governing class that is adept in the shrewd use of chicanery, fraud, corruption; and in the highest degree difficult to overthrow such a class when it successfully assimilates most of the individuals in the subject class who show those same talents, are adept in those same arts, and might therefore become the leaders of such plebeians as are disposed to use violence. Thus left without leadership, without talent, disorganized, the subject class is almost always powerless to set up any lasting regime. 3. So the combination-residues (Class I) become to some extent enfeebled in the subject class.[34]

Here, Pareto's analysis bears many similarities with Mosca's in terms of the fact that the elite are constantly replenished by exceptional individuals from the lower classes, and risk overthrow if they are too exclusive. However, if foxes manage to create a situation where the elite hoover up all the foxes in a society, the lions will find it difficult to organise. One might argue that this has been the case in the liberal democracies of the USA and Europe since 1945 in which foxes have overwhelmingly predominated in the elite and the non-governing elite has greatly expanded to encompass practically all of the Class 1 type individuals in society. Only recently have we seen the elites of Western nations starting to deliberately exclude exceptional Class 1 type individuals from its ranks in the name of its humanitarian doctrines. If Pareto is correct, this would suggest a shift back to a predominance of lions in the coming years once there is a critical mass of excluded Class 1 types to lead them. However, as in Mosca, this process is seen from afar in Pareto, and it would be up to Robert Michels, whom we will consider in the next chapter, to bring

34   Pareto, *The Mind and Society*, vol 4, §2179, pp. 1516–17.

the analysis down to the level of the individual organisation.

Pareto's *The Mind and Society*, even taken in an abridged form, remains a formidable challenge for any reader today—'monstrous' remains an apt description.[35] We do not have to accept his entire sociology to see the value in his insights. For example, it strikes me that in his zeal to strip his own worldview of any metaphysical content, Pareto too readily dismissed ideologies as second-order effects and seems to overlook their tremendous animating spirit. On this score, Mosca—less wedded to the totality of a system—was a much shrewder observer of history. Myths are not simply 'beautiful lies' used to hoodwink the masses, but also extremely powerful motivators of human action, which Pareto reduces 'to be minor and for the most part indirect'.[36] Even in the most charitable interpretation, where the power of myth to motivate is admitted but then attributed to the strength of an underlying sentiment, Pareto must still explain away wars fought over clashes of belief to *some other cause*. Still, he has the insight that humans have a deep need for such myths, that there will never be a time when they are not generated, that they are justified because humans also have a need for rationalisation, and at the same time because these are simply 'needs', what is generated and justified is seldom, if ever, rational. This we can accept without denying myths as a major causal factor in historical change. Likewise, while we may quibble about primary causal factors, the fundamental notion of the circulation of the elites, the categories of foxes and lions, and idea of elite *composition*—including the exclusivity or inclusivity of that elite—remains of great value to the student of politics and history.

---

35   Vilfredo Pareto, quoted in Bellamy, *Modern Italian Social Theory*, p. 25.
36   Burnham, *The Machiavellians*, p. 152.

Chapter 4

THE IRON LAW OF OLIGARCHY AND ORGANISATIONAL STRUCTURE

Robert Michels published *Political Parties* in 1911, which was translated into English in 1915. He also had personal and professional relationships with both Pareto and Mosca which forms the actual, as well as theoretical, link between the three thinkers for them to be classed as 'The Italian School of Elitism'. He knew Pareto from his time in Paris and through correspondence about Georges Sorel, for whom they held a mutual admiration. Michels knew Mosca from his time in Turin where he studied and taught in the first decade of the 1900s. In fact, Mosca seems to have taken Michels, eighteen years his junior, under his wing—to the extent that he was described as a 'mentor-like figure' to him;[1] Michels has even been described straightforwardly as 'Mosca's pupil',[2] or 'Mosca's disciple'.[3] It is well known that Mosca and Pareto did not like each other. The chief source of the animosity is that Mosca believed he should have been recognised as the

1   Ettore A. Albertoni, *Mosca and the Theory of Elitism*, trans. Paul Goodrick (Oxford: Blackwell, 1987), p. 6.
2   Richard Bellamy, *Modern Italian Social Theory* (Oxford: Blackwell, 1987), p. 135.
3   Geraint Parry, *Political Elites* (London: George Allen and Unwin, 1971), p. 42.

originator of the theory of elites, which Pareto did not acknowledge. Therefore, 'to come to be regarded by both as a
kind of disciple was no mean feat'.[4] 'Michels found himself
in a difficult position when he tried to give credit to both
men, whom he liked and respected as intellectual mentors.'[5]
Perhaps because he acknowledged his intellectual debts, Michels has often been seen as 'a considerable synthesizer of the
ideas of others',[6] and as the 'least original among the trio of
neo-Machiavellians'.[7] In truth, 'originality' is not and should
not be seen as a criteria by which to judge elite theorists, but
rather the degree to which their works describe reality. In
any case, 'in putting forward a detailed mechanism through
which his "law" operates, Michels does make an important
advance on the work of Mosca and Pareto.'[8]

In *Political Parties*, Robert Michels largely takes for granted the lessons of Mosca and Pareto, especially as they per-
tain to the impossibility of democracy. 'For the will of the
people is not transferrable, nor even the will of the single
individual', argues Michels, drawing on Mosca directly, 'in
actual fact, directly [sic] the election is finished, the power of the mass over the delegate comes to an end.' Hence
not only is direct democracy impossible, but also *representative* democracy is necessarily a fiction. 'To represent, in
this sense, comes to mean that the purely individual desire masquerades and is accepted as the will of the mass.'[9]
'The rank and file are manipulated into accepting policies

4   David Beetham, 'Michels and His Critics', *European Journal of
Sociology*, 22:1 (January 1981), p. 82.
5   H. Stuart Hughes, *Consciousness and Society* (Brighton: The Harvester Press, 1979), p. 255.
6   Beetham, 'Michels and His Critics', p. 82.
7   Hughes, *Consciousness and Society*, p. 272.
8   Gordon Hands, 'Roberto Michels and the Study of Political
Parties', *British Journal of Political Science*, 1:2 (April 1971), p. 157.
9   Robert Michels, *Political Parties: A Sociology of the Oligarchical
Tendencies of Modern Democracy* (1915; New York: The Free Press,
1962), pp. 73–4, 76, 77.

with which they would not otherwise agree, and which are not in their interests, or at least are primarily in the interests of the leadership group.'[10] However, what is new in Michels is the fact that he applies this analysis not simply at the level of the state but to *all organisations*: '[large] families, totems, tribes, cities, nations, empires, churches, economic classes, clubs, parties', which are 'an altogether universal feature of human life.'[11] Since people invariably organise themselves into groups and since none but the smallest groups are truly democratic in the sense of truly representing the interests of their members:

> Organization implies a tendency to oligarchy. In every organization, whether it be a political party, a professional union, or any other association of any kind, the aristocratic tendency manifests itself very clearly. [...] As a result of organization, every party or professional union becomes divided into a minority of directors and a majority of directed.[12]

Thus, one could gain institutional control simply by capturing the directorship of the organization. Change would flow top-down as against the individual wills of the disorganized majority. This is Michels's famous *iron law of oligarchy*. Geraint Parry gives a succinct formulation of the law: 'In any organization of any size leadership becomes necessary to its success and survival. The nature of organization is such that it gives power and advantages to the group of leaders who cannot then be checked or held accountable by their followers.'[13] Michels himself put it even more succinctly: 'Who says organization, says oligarchy'.[14]

10   Hands, 'Roberto Michels and the Study of Political Parties', p. 160.
11   James Burnham, *The Machiavellians: Defenders of Freedom* (London: Putnam, 1943), p. 99.
12   Michels, *Political Parties*, p. 70.
13   Parry, *Political Elites*, pp. 42–3.
14   Michels, *Political Parties*, p. 365.

What does Michels mean by 'organization' and what does he mean by 'oligarchy'? C. W. Cassinelli was keen to strip the iron law of any ambiguity and so sought to define these terms more tightly: 'An organization is a group of human activities ordered by a system of specialization of function; a sub-group of these activities has as its goal the maintenance of this order or of an order very similar to it.'[15] He also defines 'oligarchy' as follows: 'An oligarchy is an organization characterized by the fact that part of the activities of which it consists, viz., the activities having the highest degree of authority (which have been called "leadership" or "executive" activities), are free from control by any of the remainder of the organizational activities. This concept leads to a generalization which might be called "a theory of irresponsible leadership."'[16] This does not mean that the leadership can simply ignore the mass—they must anticipate the reactions of the led—but rather that given the limitations of the raw materials with which they have to work, they have free rein to do whatever they want.

Incidentally, the iron law of oligarchy explains, at a stroke, why the 'Long March' of the Left through the institutions since 1945 in both America and across Europe has been so effective. They never needed to persuade most people in the populace or even at an organizational level of their view, they simply needed to capture the leadership positions to impose their will. The typical student at a university is not an activist, they are mostly disinterested—as Michels says of young trade union members, 'they are heedless, their thoughts run in erotic channels, they are always hoping some miracle will deliver them from the need of passing their whole lives as simple wage-earn-

15   C. W. Cassinelli, 'The Law of Oligarchy', *The American Political Science Review*, 47:3 (September 1957), p. 777.
16   Cassinelli, 'The Law of Oligarchy', p. 779.

ers'[17]—but the leadership of the Student Union is not. In every university, therefore, the will of the Student Union Leadership will prevail on campus. If that will is to enforce a quasi-Marxist progressive hegemony, then that will be the case too, on every campus. And so, we might see how 'society' might wake up one day to find that it has sleep-walked into a quasi-Marxist progressive hegemony. The hard 'check' on this is that the mass will not tolerate *intrusive* interventions into their everyday lives. Let us imagine the leadership of a Student Union sought to ban meat on campus in the name of their political agenda—in such circumstances one might imagine a *rapid* and *organised* response from outraged students who do not wish to have vegetarianism imposed on them—and the Student Union would likely experience its own 'circulation of elites'. However, the leadership would *know* this limitation and likely not push so far as to deprive themselves of power. In other words, if they are canny, the leaders will take what they can get away with and no more.

There are a few features of Michels's analysis that should be stressed. He identifies five factors that prove his iron law: two psychological and three practical. Let us deal with the two psychological factors first. Much like Pareto, Michels does not ignore psychology. In fact, he considers both the psychology of the masses and the leaders. As regards the former, in an analysis which chiefly seems to be derived from Gustave Le Bon,[18] he notes 'the "psychological need" for leadership felt by the masses, their predisposition to hero-worship, and their tendency to excessive gratitude.'[19] 'People *en masse* are subject to waves of emotion which spread like a contagious disease, and they are

17   Michels, *Political Parties.*, p. 105.
18   Gustave Le Bon, *The Crowd: A Study of the Popular Mind* (1897; Greenville, SC: Traders Press, 1994).
19   Hands, 'Roberto Michels and the Study of Political Parties', p. 162.

readily manipulated by leaders skilled in demagogy and knowledgeable in the workings of the collective psyche.'[20] As regards the psychology of the leaders, however, we get something approaching Lord Acton's maxim that 'absolute power corrupts absolutely'[21]:

> The consciousness of power always produces vanity, an undue belief in personal greatness. The desire to dominate, for good or for evil, is universal. These are elementary psychological facts. In the leader, the consciousness of his personal worth, and of the need which the mass feels for guidance, combine to induce in his mind a recognition of his own superiority (real or supposed), and awake, in addition, that spirit of command which exists in the germ of every man and woman. We see from this that every human power seeks to enlarge its prerogatives. He who has acquired power will almost always endeavour to consolidate it and to extend it, to multiply the ramparts which defend his position, and to withdraw himself from the control of the masses.[22]

Thus, once a leader has attained power in the first place, they are driven by something like a Nietzschean Will to Power, they are intoxicated by it and want more of it. It is significant that it is *power* that is the motivation and not merely money. All too often, naïve analyses of elites imagine they are motivated by profits: this is almost never the case. The prospect of *control* is a far greater motivator than *greed*.

Let us turn now to the three factors of practicality which ensure the iron law of oligarchy. The problem is not simply one of psychology, which is to say the selfishness of the leaders in pursuing their own interests instead of those of

20   Beetham, 'Michels and His Critics', p. 83.
21   John Emerich Edward Dalberg-Acton, 'Acton-Creighton Correspondence', in *Essays on Freedom and Power*, ed. Gertrude Himmelfarb (Glencoe, IL: The Free Press, 1948), p. 364.
22   Michels, *Political Parties*, p. 206.

the masses, but also one of practical necessity. It is, as Samuel T. Francis might put it, a problem of 'mass and scale'.[23] 'Large, organizationally complex associations, compared with small, simple associations,'[24] for *mechanical, technical* and *tactical* reasons must succumb to the organisational, and therefore, the oligarchical principle. First, the *mechanical* reason is that—when dealing with organizations that number in the thousands, or even hundreds of thousands, or millions—you physically cannot get all the people in the same room at the same time. Even voting mechanisms are frustrated by the fact that, when dealing with that many people, you need to narrow their choices down to just a few of the most sensible suggestions. Even then, most people simply lack the time and interest to partake in constant referenda. From his time seeing the Social Democratic Party of Germany in practice, Michels saw that 'committees set-up to organise the day-to-day running of the party were systematically unattended.'[25] Because of this, the democratic principle must give way to the oligarchical principle purely on mechanical grounds. However, let us pretend that there was a way—perhaps using modern technology and some crowd-sourcing algorithm—to overcome the mechanical issue, there remains the *technical* one. 'There are innumerable bureaucratic details that must be seen to if the organization is to be kept alive. There are financial, administrative, diplomatic problems to be settled.'[26] 'A political party campaigning for power needs to organize its vote, canvass supporters, supply information for speakers, raise contributions, attend to the party's fi-

23   Samuel T. Francis, *Leviathan and Its Enemies* (Arlington, VA: Washing Summit Publishers, 2016), p. 9.
24   John D. May, 'Democracy, Organization, Michels', *The American Political Science Review*, 59:2 (June 1965), p. 417.
25   Hugo Drochon, 'Robert Michels, The Iron Law of Oligarchy and Dynamic Democracy', *Constellations* 27 (2020), p. 187.
26   Burnham, *The Machiavellians*, p. 104.

nancial structure and its legal standing. It needs to establish a co-ordinated policy line for the sake of consistency and solidarity.'[27] However, there is yet a third reason
that the organisational principle prevails, even beyond the
technical requirements, which is *tactical*: the masses simply *will not and cannot organise*. At times, Michels seems to
write as if the masses possess some pathological need to be
led. For example, he writes:

> The most striking proof of the organic weakness of
> the mass is furnished by the way in which, when de-
> prived of the leaders in time of action, they abandon
> the field of battle in disordered flight; they seem to
> have no power of instinctive reorganization, and are
> useless until new captains arise capable of replacing
> those that have been lost.[28]

A crowd without organised leadership will simply devolve
into a rabble. It is difficult not to think of the so-called 'Storm-
ing of the Capitol' on 6th January 2021. Donald Trump having
gathered his 'masses' in Washington DC, simply abandoned
them and they devolved to a disorganised mob, with no direction or purpose. Once inside the Capitol building all the
individuals involved could think to do was inanely take pic-
tures of themselves with their mobile phones. There was no
plan, no coordination, no leadership. Michels would have
predicted that it would have turned out as it did. And this is
the *tactical* reason for the iron law.

Since there is no escaping the iron law of oligarchy, in
any political party, power accrues to the bureaucrats who
manage these things and tend to be concerned more with
practical techniques than with principle. One might think
of the power of political Svengalis such as Alistair Campbell in the British New Labour administration or, more
recently, Dominic Cummings. Secondarily, power accrues

---

27   Parry, *Political Elites*, p. 43.
28   Michels, *Political Parties*, p. 90.

to the elected representatives whose source of power lies outside the party itself in the voter-base. We therefore see again the two strata of elites identified by Mosca and Pareto: we might call the former, the *bureaucracy* of the party, the "non-governing elite", and the latter, the actual politicians, the "governing elite". Sometimes we might see someone with the skills of the former transition to becoming one of the latter, as was the case with Peter Mandelson when he became elected as an MP for Labour in 1992 after being their 'Director of Communications'. Still, Mandelson's skills as an organiser were utilised even once he became an MP. A testament to this fact is that even after having stepped down as an MP, in 2008 Prime Minister Gordon Brown so required Mandelson's *technical* skills that he made him a Lord and brought him back into the cabinet.[29] One of the consequences of this power that accrues to the leaders is that it manifests in what James Burnham called 'customary right':

> Formally, a new election for an office may be held every year or two. But, in practice, the mere fact that an individual has held the office in the past is thought by him and by the members to give him a moral claim on it for the future; or, if not on the same office, then on some other leadership post in the organization. It becomes almost unthinkable that those who have served the organization so well, or even not so well, in the past should be thrown aside. [...] If the vagaries of elections by chance turn out wrong, then a niche is found in an embassy or bureau or post-office, or, at the end, in the pension list.[30]

This is partly what Michels means when he says, 'Power is

29   Jon Swaine, 'Peter Mandelson profile: The Prince of Darkness Returns', Daily Telegraph (3 October 2008): https://www.telegraph.co.uk/news/politics/labour/3127802/Peter-Mandelson-profile-The-Prince-of-Darkness-returns.html.

30   Burnham, *The Machiavellians*, p. 106.

always conservative.' The interests of the leaders turn from any principled political stance they might have held to the business of maintaining positions of power. To become 'stable and irremovable'.[31] He points to the leadership of the supposedly anti-war, anti-patriotic Social Democratic Party of Germany magically becoming pro-war, and pro-patriotic on the eve of World War I. We might think of other, more recent, examples. In Britain, the Liberal Democrats under Nick Clegg campaigned to abolish university tuition fees only to form a coalition with the Conservatives. Then, as part of the coalition government, they *raised* tuition fees from £3,290 to £9,000 per year.[32] While voters did not forget the betrayal, a study of the personal fortunes of Liberal Democrat leaders from that era would be instructive in proving Michels's point. Nick Clegg went on to be Vice-President for Global Affairs and Communications of Facebook, Inc; Vince Cable became the new party leader before retiring; Menzies Campbell was made a Lord; David Laws became the Chief Executive of the Education Policy Institute; Simon Hughes was knighted and made Chancellor of London South Bank University along with at least seven other senior advisory or directorial roles. British politicians have a remarkable capacity to 'fail upwards'. These politicians may have been voted out of their seats, but they remained part of the ruling class and enlarged the scope of their personal power.

The leaders of political parties maintain power—according to Michels—by virtue of the practicalities of organisation. Hugo Drochon summarises what these are:

> There are three different resources that, according to Michels, ensure the leaders keep control of their party. These are as follows: (a) Officials have superior knowledge, in that they are privy to much in-

31   Michels, *Political Parties*, pp. 333, 364.
32   Sean Coughlin, 'Students Face Tuition Fees Rising to £9,000', BBC News (3 November 2010): https://www.bbc.co.uk/news/education-11677862.

formation that can be used to secure assent for their programme; (b) they control the formal means of communication, because they dominate the organisation's press (parties still had their own newspapers at the time), and as full-time salaried officials, they can travel from place to place presenting their case at the organisation's expense, where their position enables them to command an audience; and (c), they have skill in the art of politics, in that they are far more adept than nonprofessionals in making speeches, writing articles and organising group activities.[33]

Political leaders therefore enjoy an advantage in *knowledge, communication methods,* and *political skills* over the mass in whom, as we have already seen, Michels considers all three resources to be totally lacking. This offers a great advance over Marxist analysis which posits that leaders only enjoy their positions by virtue of ownership of the means of production. Michels is suggesting that it is the *abilities* of the leaders to organise through these three resources that justifies and maintains their position. This will become significant when we come to consider James Burnham's *The Managerial Revolution*, because in this are the seeds for the takeover of managers and bureaucrats. If *organisational ability* rather than land or business ownership is the criterion by which leaders are chosen, then it stands to reason that the managers would come to challenge and displace the power of the bourgeoisie, just as the bourgeoisie displaced the old aristocracies. However, in both Mosca and Michels, the role of 'the rich' is somewhat hazy. It is certainly the case that wealth can be used to buy influence and power, but it is not clear whether the fact of ownership can trump the practical realities of organisation. When Michels broaches this topic, he talks mainly about the extent to which old leaders are distrustful of and often unwilling to cede power to new upstarts which

---

33   Drochon, 'Robert Michels, The Iron Law of Oligarchy and Dynamic Democracy', p. 188.

frequently leads to censorship and a curbing of free speech.[34] Again it seems that organisation is the *decisive* factor, even if wealth can grant certain advantages.

Issues of wealth aside, the tactics of old leaders against young aspirants are interesting in and of themselves. Michels notes that the old leaders have many tactical advantages over the young aspirants, such as the fact that they have responsibilities of which the aspirants are free and therefore can always call them 'irresponsible'. He also notes that the old leaders will style themselves as the sensible people, the 'adults in the room' against 'extremists' whom they can paint as naïvely idealist or as demagogues, and in this they can rely on the natural conservatism of the masses in the party membership (who distrust newcomers) to enlist support. They will then point to this support to enforce 'discipline and subordination' on the upstarts.[35] In the early 2020s, one might think of the ancient leaders of the US Democratic Party, such as Joe Biden, Nancy Pelosi, Chuck Schumer and Elizabeth Warren, fending off young aspirants in Alexandria Ocasio-Cortez, Rashida Tlaib, Ayanna Pressley and Ilhan Omar collectively known as 'the Squad'. The Democrat old guard have to date employed virtually every trick that Michels describes against the young aspirants. In this chapter, Michels adds a lot of colour and detail to Pareto's circulation of elites. In Mosca and Pareto, the analysis is often 'zoomed out', at a level of remove, but in Michels we see the human faces. This is because he is looking at smaller units of organization than the state but let us not forget that the mass organization is merely 'a state in miniature'.[36]

The value of Michels is in his many insights into practical, 'on-the-ground' politics and the realities of organisation. His chief contribution is to see that what Mosca and Pareto had said on the level of whole countries, is also true at the level of

---

34   Michels, *Political Parties*, pp. 176–7.
35   Michels, *Political Parties*, pp. 179, 177.
36   Hands, 'Roberto Michels and the Study of Political Parties', p. 170.

large organisations. However, because his analysis is focused on individual organisations in microcosm, he does not give us—crucially—the relationships *between* organisations or how leaders in one organisation respond to leaders in external organisations who are no *direct threat* to them. Is the tendency of elites in disparate organisations to diverge in rivalrous competition or to converge as people with largely similar interests and goals? Recall, for example, Nick Clegg leaving the Liberal Democrat Party to join Facebook. Are the interests of the Liberal Democrats and Facebook aligned or in competition? These questions would be left for James Burnham and Samuel T. Francis to flesh out and we can return to them later. For now, I will say in passing that Mosca gives us the categories of 'feudal' and 'bureaucratic' with which to think about this problem on a state level. If large institutions in disparate fields—for example a political party and a corporation—become more rivalrous, it is a sign of feudalisation, which is to say *competing* power centres. If they are on the opposite trajectory, towards convergence, we might say it is a sign of bureaucratization or even, in Mosca's phrase, 'over- bureaucratization'.[37] Michels provides a whole chapter himself on this topic called 'Bureaucracy. Centralizing and Decentralizing Tendencies,'[38] but this offers no significant advance on Mosca and finds itself too bogged down in the minutiae of the contemporary German socialist scene of 1911. He does complain entertainingly, however, about the problem of bureaucratic specialisation leading to mundane, career-seeking, obsequious men who know nothing of bigger ideas or principles. Bureaucratization 'suppresses individuality and gives to the society in which employees predominate a narrow petty-bourgeois and philistine stamp. The bureaucratic spirit corrupts character and engenders moral poverty.'[39] Thus

37   Gaetano Mosca, *The Ruling Class*, ed. Arthur Livingston, trans. Hannah D. Khan (1895; New York: McGraw-Hill, 1939), p. 215.
38   Michels, *Political Parties*, pp. 188–202.
39   Michels, *Political Parties*, p. 191.

within bureaucratization is a degenerative principle—degenerative in the general quality of the personnel who form the non-governing elite—that could sow the seeds of a move towards decentralization by generating disaffected but more 'visionary' types who agitate for change. We can see in this something of Pareto's circulation of elites. This also has the seed of an idea that would be dubbed 'Bioleninism' by the blogger Spandrell in 2018,[40] whereby these key bureaucratic roles are filled based more on loyalty to the party than for their actual skills. In Michels's terms what is really happening is that they are weakening one of the key pillars on which the iron law depends: the *practical abilities* of the leaders to organise. If too many mundane specialists become toadying sycophants, then the advantage of the leaders is lost.

The great strength of Michels's analysis, at the level of the organisation, is that it is never monocausal: he always stresses *both* the psychological and practical factors, which combine to make his law 'iron'. Much of the secondary scholarship on Michels seems irritated that his theory is not neater and confused by the fact that he calls it 'iron'.[41] It is 'iron' because there is no escape from it, even *if* you resolved the psychological factors, you would still have to deal with the practical factors and vice versa. They are also mutually reinforcing, which is to say that the practical factors *compound* the psychological factors and vice versa—the more a person stays in power, the more knowledge and practical skills they gain, the more they *want* to stay in power. By the same token, the more a person remains a mere plebian, the less knowledge and experience of practical organisation they gain, and the more *reliant*—both practically and psychologically—they become on the leaders. As we have seen, the law is 'iron' also in the sense that the psychological factors are twofold: both

40   Spandrell, 'Leninism and Bioleninism', Bloody Shovel 3 (21 January 2018): https://spandrell.com/2017/11/14/biological-leninism/.

41   See, for example, Hands, 'Roberto Michels and the Study of Political Parties', p. 158.

the leaders and the masses. Even *if* you solved the problem of selfish leaders, you still have the problem of the helpless masses. The practical factors are even more robust: mechanical, technical, and tactical underlined and maintained by the leaders' resources of knowledge, communication methods, and political skills. The mass thus must overcome at least six near-insurmountable hurdles to overturn the 'iron law' which is practically impossible. The only method by which it is possible to displace the leadership within a party is to form a new leadership and out-manoeuvre the old one in these six categories—still no easy task since they have every motivation to stop you—but at least possible.

Chapter 5
SOVEREIGNTY,
FRIENDS AND ENEMIES

Carl Schmitt is arguably the most important political and legal theorist of the Twentieth Century. He produced a large
body of work and the secondary literature that has been
produced on Schmitt could fill a small library. Much like the
elite theorists, his analysis of power and politics was above
all else realist, describing things as they are and not how they
ought to be. Here I will focus only on his two most famous
ideas: 'sovereign is he who decides on the exception',[1] and
'the specific political distinction to which political actions and
motives can be reduced is that between friend and enemy.'[2]
These are found in his two booklets *Political Theology* (1922)
and *The Concept of the Political* (1932), which were his fourth
and twelfth major publications respectively. I will be using
the standard scholarly editions of these works, but they have
been helpfully collected in *The Sovereign Collection* by Antelope Hill which makes a virtue of its lack of commentary or
apologia.[3] While many of the thinkers we have considered

1   Carl Schmitt, *Political Theology: Four Chapters on the Concept of
Sovereignty*, trans. George Schwab (1922; Chicago, IL: University of
Chicago Press, 2005), p. 5.
2   Carl Schmitt, *The Concept of the Political*, trans. George Schwab
(1932; Chicago, IL: University of Chicago Press, 2007), p. 26.
3   Carl Schmitt, *The Sovereign Collection*, trans C.J. Miller (Quakertown, PA: Antelope Hill Publishing, 2020).

thus far have been controversial, Carl Schmitt is held responsible by some as providing the legal justification for the Nazi regime.[4] This is beyond our scope, but it is worth knowing that in the 1970s, scholars such as George Schwab made great efforts of 'de-Nazify' Schmitt,[5] and by the late 1980s the journal *Telos* had become and remains the house publication for Schmitt scholarship.[6] By the end of the 1990s, far left scholars were publishing their own book-length collections of essays on Schmitt.[7] It is testament to the power of Schmitt's clarity and the penetration of his analysis that he could overcome the ultimate stigma and be rehabilitated by mainstream scholarship in this way.

Much influenced by Thomas Hobbes, Schmitt saw the central role of governmental authority as one of maintaining order and stability. As we saw in Mosca, every ruling class must lean on a political formula to which the ruled subscribe to gain legitimacy. Even though every political formula will be rooted in claims that do not stand the test of empirical reality, as Pareto maintained, people irrationally believe them in any case despite the facts, almost as quasi-religious myths. Schmitt recognised something sim-

4   For an account of apologia for Schmitt which also emphasises his role in legitimating Adolf Hitler, see David Ohana, 'Carl Schmitt's Legal Fascism', *Politics, Religion & Ideology*, 20:3 (2019), pp. 1–28. See also, Bill Schueuerman, 'Carl Schmitt and the Nazis', German, Politics and Society, 23 (Summer 1991), pp. 71–79.

5   See George Schwab, *The Challenge of the Exception: An Introduction to the Political Ideas of Carl Schmitt Between 1921 and 1936* (1970; New York: Greenwood Press, 1989).

6   This was triggered by the vehement reactions to Ellen Kennedy, 'Carl Schmitt and the Frankfurt School', *Telos*, 71 (March 1987), pp. 37–66; and the transition of Telos becoming a Schmittian journal was announced in the following issue: G.L. Ulmen and Paul Piccone, 'Introduction to Carl Schmitt', Telos, 72 (June 1987), pp. 3–14.

7   Chantelle Mouffe (ed.), *The Challenge of Carl Schmitt* (New York and London: Verso, 1999).

ilar and called it 'political theology'. He argued:

> All significant concepts of the modern theory of the
> state are secularized theological concepts not only
> because of their historical development—in which
> they were transferred from theology to the theory
> of the state, whereby, for example, the omnipotent
> God became the omnipotent lawgiver—but also be-
> cause of their systematic structure, the recognition
> of which is necessary for a sociological consideration
> of these concepts. The exception in jurisprudence is
> analogous to the miracle in theology. Only by being
> aware of this analogy can we appreciate the manner
> in which the philosophical ideas of the state devel-
> oped in the last centuries.[8]

Perhaps this is why it rang so true when Herbert Spencer re-
ferred derisively to 'the divine right of parliaments' in 1884.[9]
But we must separate the issue of *legitimacy*, which concerns
consent of the ruled and the right of the rulers to rule, from
that of *sovereignty*, which concerns who has functional *authority* in a state.

In terms of sovereignty, Schmitt shows that there is
substantially no difference between systems of absolutist monarchy, such as those supported by 'throne and al-
tar' reactionaries such as Joseph de Maistre, and modern
parliamentary systems with their supposed separation of
powers. This will likely appear absurd to some. How could
an absolutist monarch bear any relation to, for example,
the US government with its careful system of checks and
balances, its separation of the executive from the legisla-
ture and judiciary and so on? The answer lies in the fact
that Schmitt saw it fit to judge any political system not by
its *norms* but when it was *under crisis*.

This was not a new move in the history of political the-

8   Schmitt, *Political Theology*, p. 36.
9   Herbert Spencer, *The Man versus The State* (1884; Indianapolis,
IN: Liberty Fund, 1982), p. 123.

ory. For example, in *An Enquiry Concerning the Principles of Morals* (1751), David Hume asked: 'Is it any crime, after a shipwreck, to seize whatever means or instrument of safety one can lay hold of, without regard to the former limitations of property?'[10] Hume imagines a city under siege whose inhabitants were in danger of perishing with hunger, or a civil war. In such conditions we expect the normal laws of justice to be suspended, because they no longer serve any purpose. It is here Schmitt would interject with his two favourite questions: 'who decides?' (*quis judicabit?*), 'who interprets?' (*quis interpretabitur?*). And hence his famous dictum: 'sovereign is he who decides on the exception'. He says:

> Precisely a philosophy of concrete life must not withdraw from the exception and the extreme case, but must be interested in it to the highest degree. The exception can be more important to it than the rule, not because of a romantic irony for the paradox, but because the seriousness of an insight goes deeper than the clear generalizations inferred from what ordinarily repeats itself. The exception is more interesting than the rule. The rule proves nothing; the exception proves everything: It confirms not only the rule but also its existence, which derives only from the exception. In the exception the power of real life breaks through the crust of a mechanism that has become torpid by repetition.[11]

We may consider, for example, the issue of the US Election of 2020, which was disputed by its official loser, Donald Trump, who alleged that his opponent, Joe Biden, had engaged in widescale fraud. This showed an amazed global audience the US system under *crisis*. The Supreme Court would hear no

---

10   David Hume, *An Enquiry Concerning the Principles of Morals*, ed. J.B. Schneewind (1751; Indianapolis, IN: Hackett Publishing, 1983), 3.1, p. 20.

11   Schmitt, *Political Theology*, p. 15.

cases and officially would review no evidence; it ruled that Texas and seventeen other States had 'no standing'. Over 7,000 sworn affidavits alleging fraud were effectively ignored by the American legal system—and that was in Michigan alone.[12] We need only entertain a counterfactual: what if the charges had been the other way around? In fact, we glimpsed what that may have looked like in the Russiagate fiasco which dogged Trump's presidency and mired it in legal challenges, indictments, FBI special investigations and so on for nearly his entire term. The chief claims of Russiagate, which were loudly amplified by the media, were subsequently proven to have been fabricated during an investigation by FBI Special Counsel John Durham with two indictments to date at the time of writing.[13] However, by this time, after the fact, neither the media nor the public cared. A Schmittian analysis of these details would show us three things: first, Donald Trump, despite holding the office of US President, never had sovereignty; second, whoever *is* sovereign in the United States—which one suspects is neither Joe Biden nor the Supreme Court—did not like Donald Trump very much and sought to make him an exception; third, there is no sovereignty in 'the people' whatsoever and the preamble of the US Constitution, 'We the People', is an empty slogan.

While the elite theorists sought chiefly to attack democracy as a sham, Schmitt's main target was liberalism which he believed constantly sought to obscure and obfuscate power behind legal fictions. 'For Schmitt the sov-

12   Scott McCallen, 'Over 7,000 Affidavits Delivered to Michigan Lawmakers Claim Election Fraud', Washington Examiner (18 June 2021): https://www.washingtonexaminer.com/politics/over-7-000-affidavits-delivered-to-michigan-lawmakers-claim-election-fraud; Daniel Villarreal, 'RNC Chair Says People Have Come Forward With 11,000 Voter Fraud Claims', Newsweek (11 November 2020): https://www.newsweek.com/rnc-chair-says-11000-people-have-come-forward-voter-fraud-claims-1546546.
13   See https://www.justice.gov/sco-durham.

ereign authority not only was bound to the normally valid legal order but also transcended it. [...] his sovereign slumbers in normal times but suddenly awakens when a normal situation threatens to become an exception. [...] In this critical moment sovereign power reveals itself in its purest form.'[14] It stands to reason, then, that because the sovereign decides the exception, he is not subject to the law. In fact, the sovereign not only decides the exception but also *decides when order and stability are restored.* It may surprise some people to learn that the United States has been in a near continuous state of National Emergency since 1917.[15] Emergency Executive Orders dating back to the Jimmy Carter administration are still active. Powers invoked by George W. Bush to fight his 'War on Terror' were never rescinded.[16] In the UK, the Coronavirus Act 2020 granted the government sweeping and unprecedented emergency powers over its subjects in a remit that extended far beyond the treatment of people infected with COVID-19, which include powers to detain 'potentially infectious persons'; powers to prevent mass gatherings; mass surveillance powers; and the imposition of criminal sanctions for disease transmission.[17] The initial indictment

14   George Schwab, 'Introduction', in *Political Theology*, pp. xliii–xliv.

15   For a book-length study on this see Alain de Benoist, *Carl Schmitt Today: Terrorism, 'Just War' and the State of Emergency* (London: Arktos Media, 2013).

16   Brennan Center for Justice, 'A Guide to Emergency Powers and Their Use' (24 April 2020): https://www.brennancenter.org/our-work/research-reports/guide-emergency-powers-and-their-use. See especially this table: https://www.brennancenter.org/sites/default/files/analysis/NEA%20Declarations.pdf.

17   Maximillian Shreeve-McGiffen, 'The Coronavirus Act 2020: Unprecedented Powers, But Are They Necessary?', *The Oxford University Undergraduate Law Journal* (7 May 2020): https://www.law.ox.ac.uk/ouulj/blog/2020/05/coronavirus-act-2020-unprecedented-powers-are-they-necessary.

of Julian Assange in 2018 rested on the authority of Executive Order 13526 issued by President Barack Obama in 2009 which defined what counts as a 'Secret',[18] although he was later charged with seventeen further charges each of which carry a ten-year sentence.[19] Viewed in this way, it is easier to understand Schmitt's insistence on looking at the exception rather than the theoretical norm. In *theory*, there is a legal norm, but in *practice*, we are nearly constantly in the exception. As Schmitt put it: 'All law is "situational law." The sovereign produces and guarantees the situation in its totality. He has the monopoly over this last decision. Therein resides the essence of the state's sovereignty, which must be juristically defined correctly, not as the monopoly to coerce or to rule, but as the monopoly to decide.'[20]

This is the basis for Schmitt's doctrine of 'decisionism'. To better understand this, let us consider a lengthy passage in which he compares de Maistre to various anarchists:

> De Maistre spoke with particular fondness of sovereignty, which essentially meant decision. To him the relevance of the state rested on the fact that it provided a decision, the relevance of the Church on its rendering of the last decision that could not be appealed. Infallibility was for him the essence of the decision that cannot be appealed, and the infallibility of the spiritual order was of the same nature as the sover-

18   'United States v. Julian Paul Assange', Criminal No. 1:18-cr-l 11 (CMH): https://www.justice.gov/opa/press-release/file/1153486/download?utm_medium=email&utm_source=govdelivery/

19   Kevin Breuninger and Dan Mangan, 'WikiLeaks' Julian Assange charged with 17 new criminal counts, including violating Espionage Act', CNBC (23 May 2019): https://www.cnbc.com/2019/05/23/wikileaks-co-founder-julian-assange-charged-with-17-new-criminal-counts.html.

20   Schmitt, *Political Theology*, p. 13.

eignty of the state order. The two words infallibility and sovereignty were perfectly synonymous. To him, every sovereignty acted as if it were infallible, every government was absolute—a sentence that an anarchist could pronounce verbatim, even if his intention was an entirely different one. In this sentence there lies the clearest antithesis in the entire history of political ideas. All the anarchist theories from Babeuf to Bakunin, Kropotkin, and Otto Gross revolve around the one axiom: 'The people are good, but the magistrate is corruptible.' De Maistre asserted the exact opposite, namely, that authority as such is good once it exists: 'Any government is good once it is established,' the reason being that a decision is inherent in the mere existence of a governmental authority, and the decision as such is in turn valuable precisely because, as far as the most essential issues are concerned, making a decision is more important than how a decision is made. 'It is definitely not in our interest that a question be decided in one way or another but that it be decided without delay and without appeal.' In practice, not to be subject to error and not to be accused of error were for him the same. The important point was that no higher authority could review the decision.[21]

This may make it sound as if de Maistre and Schmitt are putting the sovereign beyond criticism or reproach, however they simply mean that *in practice* sovereignty rests on 'decisionism'. Note that this thinking is also present in Pareto's 'man of action'. If the sovereign is arbitrary or corrupt or tyrannical, he will fail to uphold his key obligation which is to uphold order and stability and therefore be illegitimate: 'the sovereign who cannot protect, has no right to demand obedience.'[22]

George Schwab formalised Schmitt's theory in the fol-

---

21   Schmitt, *Political Theology*, pp. 55–6.
22   Schwab, *The Challenge of the Exception*, p. 46.

lowing diagram:[23]

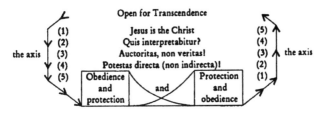

To explain this: 'Jesus is the Christ' is the political formula, this can be replaced with 'liberty, fraternity, equality', 'the will of the people', or any other empty slogan. *Quis interpretabitur?* is 'who interprets' the slogan? *Auctoritas, non veritas!* means 'authority, not truth, makes law'. *Postestas directa (non indirecta)!* means that direct power (rather than indirect power) has authority—and this is the 'axis' on which legitimate sovereignty must turn. The individual, who is at the bottom of the diagram, exchanges his obedience for protection from the sovereign. Schmitt thus showed that all power has this essentially theological and decisionist character.

Schmitt's thinking has profound and far-reaching consequences for the myths of liberalism. Let me name five of them: (1) the illusion of equality under the rule of law. As soon as we admit the exception, all pretences to such equality must be dropped. (2) that the state itself is nothing but law. 'The opponents that Schmitt stalks in the first two chapters of *Political Theology* are the proponents who advance the thesis that the state can be reduced to law, that the state is nothing but law, and that law is a total, seamless, exhaustive whole.'[24] (3) that the judiciary is neutral and impartial and somehow separate from politics. This self-evidently can never be the case, especially as the judiciary are subject to the sovereign who, by necessity, always stands above them. Franklin D. Roosevelt, one of

23   Schmitt, *Political Theology*, p. 46.
24   William Rasch, *Carl Schmitt: State and Society* (New York and London: Rowman & Littlefied, 2019), p. 54.

the few US Presidents who achieved sovereignty, not only attempted to pack the courts and pass mandatory retirement ages for justices in a bid to discipline the Supreme Court after it ruled eight of his New Deal measures unconstitutional, but also broke with convention and ran for third and fourth terms. Even if Roosevelt did not get his own way on every score, the machinations of Chief Justice Charles Evans Hughes, himself a Presidential candidate in 1916, demonstrate that the concept of a neutral apolitical judiciary is nonsense.[25] (4) the related notion that the state can ever be 'secular', which is to say devoid of a religious doctrine; there *must* be a political theology: 'Jesus is the Christ', 'liberty, fraternity, equality', 'the will of the people', 'diversity is our strength', and so on. And, therefore, (5) that no state institutions or institutions which rely on the state for their continued existence can be agnostic to the 'official faith'.

This leads naturally to Schmitt's second famous thesis: 'The concept of the state presupposes the concept of the political.' 'The specific political distinction to which political actions and motives can be reduced is that between friend and enemy.'[26] Schmitt himself saw tremendous significance in the first of these statements which opens *The Concept of the Political* as a 'Copernican moment' in state theory.[27] What did Schmitt overturn? In short, most theories of the state suppose that politics is something that takes place *within the state*, while Schmitt maintained that politics comes both *prior to and separate from the state*. Thus, politics has a 'potential to destabilize the state.'[28] If a state

25   See Jeff Shesol, *Supreme Power: Franklin Roosevelt vs. The Supreme Court* (New York: W.W. Norton, 2010).
26   Schmitt, The Concept of the Political, p. 19, 26.
27   Carl Schmitt quoted in Benjamin A. Schupmann, Carl *Schmitt's State and Constitutional Theory: A Critical Analysis* (Oxford: Oxford University Press, 2017), p. 69.
28   Schmitt, *Political Theology*, p. 79.

has genuine pretences to neutrality—as did the Weimar Republic in which he was writing—then it would be liable not only to contain great political animosity but also find itself dislodged by a political force that had no such pretences. Thus, the state *cannot* be neutral and must itself become political, which then necessitates recognising the friend-enemy distinction. By 'friend' and 'enemy', Schmitt was not talking about animosity on a personal and private level but rather on a public one:

> Even the precept 'love your enemies [...]' (*diligite inimicos vestros*) (Matt. 5:44; Luke 6:27) clearly refers to the private enemy, *inimicus,* and not the public one, *hostis.* Public enmity, according to Schmitt, is not a private matter, but in our epoch exclusively a concern of the political unit, the national sovereign state.[29]

The extreme end state of a 'public enemy' is war. At the most modest level it might be a disagreement over a tax rate. Conflicts over minor disagreements of policy do not attain the status of the *political* until they increase in intensity and become irreconcilable.

 The non-neutrality of the state might be understood more readily in the following table:

Political Theology	Friend	Enemies
Communism	Communists	Fascists, Liberals
Liberalism	Liberals	Fascists, Communists
Fascism	Fascists	Communists, Liberals

In practice, those within a political community will struggle to distinguish their enemies. Hence, it has been the practice of communists to label all their opponents 'fascists', which also increasingly became the modus operandi of social democrats, liberal democrats, and so-called neo-conservatives—many of whom were former Trotskyists—after World War

29 Schwab, *The Challenge of the Exception*, p. 51.

II.[30] In the political theology of communism, it is necessary to paint fascism as liberalism in a decayed state fighting a rearguard action in the interests of capital. Anti-Stalinist leftists, anarchists, left communists and social democrats in the 1920s and 30s, coined the phrase 'red fascism' to describe Stalin's doctrine of 'socialism in one country'.[31] In the political theology of liberalism, it was necessary to tie together communism and fascism—completely effacing their substantive differences—by viewing them as two sides of the same totalitarian (and antisemitic) coin.[32] Later it was necessary even to paint fundamentalist Islam as 'Islamofascism' which was retroactively applied as a decades 'long struggle'.[33] One neoconservative writer even attempted to coin the absurd title Liberal Fascism.[34] In the final analysis, within a liberal democracy, it is fascism that becomes the decisive and ultimate enemy rather than 'totalitarianism' or 'communism'. The experiences of Joseph McCarthy and his vilification by liberal history demonstrate that even during the Cold War, the 'enemy' was not communism per se, but rather the Soviet Bloc as a counter-hegemon and stand-in Hitler.[35] From the fascist point of view, liberals and communists allied against them in World War II. Although debates will range about whether Francisco Franco was a fascist, his enemies in the Spanish Civil War,

30   See Paul Gottfried, *Antifascism: The Course of a Crusade* (Ithaca, IL: Northern Illinois University Press, 2021).

31   A. James Gregor, *The Fascist Persuasion in Radical Politics* (Princeton, NJ: Princeton University Press, 1974), p. 193.

32   Most famously in Hannah Arendt, *The Origins of Totalitarianism* (1951; New York and London: Penguin, 2017).

33   Norman Podhoretz, *World War IV: The Long Struggle Against Islamofascism* (New York: Doubleday, 2007).

34   Jonah Goldberg, *Liberal Fascism: The Secret History of the Left from Mussolini to the Politics of Meaning* (New York and London: Penguin, 2009).

35   See Samuel T. Francis, 'The Evil that Men Don't Do: Joe McCarthy and the American Right', in *Beautiful Losers: Essays on the Failure of American Conservativism* (Columbia, MI: University of Missouri Press, 1994), pp. 139–51.

the Republican alliance, consisted of internationally-backed liberals, socialists and communists, while Mussolini and Hitler lent the Nationalist alliance their support.[36]

From the realist perspective of Schmitt, there is no *structural* difference between the liberal state, the communist state, and the fascist state—or indeed any other state. The only difference is the extent to which a regime may obscure the nature of its power or else genuinely buy into myths of neutrality. Viewed in this way, a state wedded to liberal democracy is as 'totalitarian' as any other since, by its very nature, it will be unable to tolerate any leaders who are not always already liberal democrats. Should such leaders rise, the stalwarts of liberal democracy will perceive them as 'populists', 'fascists', 'threats to democracy', and so on. The extent of free speech, free inquiry, free thought, and so on is a liberal delusion. In fact, the range of 'allowable opinion' is always exceedingly narrow and the liberal democratic state is marked by its intolerance and spectacular inability to imagine any worldview that is not its own. The dominance of liberal political theology is total. Schmitt would not have disagreed with Oswald Spengler who wrote in *The Decline of the West*:

> England, too, discovered the ideal of a Free Press, and discovered along with it that the press serves him who owns it. It does not spread 'free' opinion—it generates it. [...]
>
> Without the reader's observing it, the paper, and himself with it, changes masters. Here also money triumphs and forces the free spirits into its service. No tamer has his animals more under his power. Unleash the people as reader-mass and it will storm through the streets and hurl itself upon the target indicated, terrifying and breaking windows; a hint to the press-staff and it will become quiet and go home. The Press

36   Paul Gottfried, *Fascism: The Career of a Concept* (Ithaca, IL: Northern Illinois University Press, 2017), p. 8.

to-day is an army with carefully organized arms and branches, with journalists as officers, and readers as soldiers. But here, as in every army, the soldier obeys blindly, and war-aims and operation-plans change without his knowledge. The reader neither knows, nor is allowed to know, the purposes for which he is used, nor even the role that he is to play. A more appalling caricature of freedom of thought cannot be imagined. Formerly a man did not dare to think freely. Now he dares, but cannot; his will to think is only a willingness to think to order, and this is what he feels as *his* liberty.[37]

As Edward Bernays would go on to say these 'are the invisible rulers who control the destinies of millions. [...] In some department of our daily lives, in which we imagine ourselves as free agents, we are ruled by dictators exercising great power.'[38] The point is that *viewed from the outside*, liberal democracy looks just as 'totalitarian' as any other regime even if it relies more on subtle persuasion, nudge techniques, and other psychological tricks than coercion to obtain its results. In Pareto's terms, liberal democracy leads to rule by foxes as opposed to lions. Liberal democracy rules, as Schmitt was later to call it, by a 'Tyranny of Values' in which anti-liberal, anti-democratic, anti-materialist thinking is beyond the pale and banished from polite society.[39] Some have been quick to point out Schmitt's cynical hypocrisy for complaining when 'the boot was on the other foot', so to speak,[40] but it is perfect-

37   Oswald Spengler, *The Decline of the West*, trans. Charles Francis Atkinson (1918–22; London: George Allen & Unwin, 1961), pp. 351, 375–6.

38   Edward Bernays, *Propaganda* (1928; New York: Ig Publishing, 2005), p. 61.

39   Carl Schmitt, *The Tyranny of Values*, ed. and trans. Simona Draghici (1967; Washington, D.C.: Plutarch Press, 1996).

40   See, for example, Blake Smith, 'Liberalism for Losers: Carl Schmitt's "The Tyranny of Values"', American Affairs, 5.1 (Spring 2021): https://americanaffairsjournal.org/2021/02/liberalism-for-

ly consistent with his friend-enemy distinction: when friends are in power and imposing their values, *that is good*, when enemies are in power and imposing theirs, *that is bad*. This is politics, war by another name. As Paul Gottfried argues, 'Schmitt wishes us to know that no amount of neutralization can render human relations apolitical. However earnestly we strive for a programmed and peaceful society, the political, as friend-enemy distinction, continues to resurface.'[41]

Carl Schmitt is a thoroughly realist thinker who sees through every liberal and democratic delusion; he cuts through all myths to see plainly and without embellishment the essence of power *in practice, in actu*, as opposed to in theory or in laws which are no better than sheets of inert paper. These are lessons that—much like those of the elite theorists—people are often unwilling to admit either to themselves or to others. But as Schmitt would surely recognise with Pareto, people often seek refuge in their delusions. Critiques that accuse Schmitt himself of being an authoritarian seem to miss the fact that he is suggesting that *all successful states*, including liberal democratic ones, function in the same way: sovereign power rests in the person or persons who decide the exception and who interpret the mantras of the official political theology; politics rests on the friend-enemy distinction and the state must itself be political and define its enemies.

losers-carl-schmitts-the-tyranny-of-values/.

41   Paul Gottfried, *Carl Schmitt: Politics and Theory* (New York: Greenwood Press, 1990), pp. 63–4.

Chapter 6
THE HIGH-LOW MIDDLE
MECHANISM

Bertrand de Jouvenel wrote many works over a long career, but I wish to concentrate on his most famous work, *On Power* first published in 1945. Although he should justly be ranked alongside Carl Schmitt as one of the greatest political thinkers of the twentieth century, his work was strangely neglected by Anglo-American political scientists, even as he was showered with honours in his native France.[1] This is partly because he was dismissed as an eccentric amateur who lacked empirical rigour, and partly because—like the elite theorists—Jouvenel was a severe critic of democracy, and this was unfashionable after World War II. Unlike the elite theorists, who had American champions in Arthur Livingstone and James Burnham, Jouvenel seemed to fall between the cracks and his idiosyncrasies did not align him very easily with either liberals or conservatives. For example, Roy Pierce complained that in Jouvenel's analysis 'the real and significant differences between political systems are dissolved' and that he draws a 'false analogy [...] between the New Deal in the United States and the Nazi regime in Germany'.[2] Pierce does

1   See Carl Slevin, 'Social Change and Human Values: A Study of the Thought of Bertrand de Jouvenel', *Political Studies*, 19:1 (March 1971), pp. 51–2.
2   Roy Pierce, *Contemporary French Political Thought* (Oxford: Ox-

not explain this and assumes it is self-evident as to why Jouvenel was wrong—it is not self-evident to this reader.

Like the elite theorists, Jouvenel rejected the notion that society could ever be separated from the state. Power—by which he means central sovereign authority—is a constant in human affairs. In addition, breaking with the classical liberal tradition, he rejected the idea that the economy could ever exist free of politics: 'save in a Robinson Crusoe situation, political action (as he defines it) is an essential and prior concomitant of economic activity and he explicitly rejects the supposed division between sociology and politics.'[3] This insistence that there is no escape from politics also echoes Schmitt—although I should note that Jouvenel does not quote him or any of the elite theorists. He was touching on many of the same truths though and it is at times remarkable how similar his conclusions are to those of Mosca, Pareto, Michels or, indeed, of Schmitt. Gabriele Ciampini spotted this. For example, in Jouvenel 'it seems that the voters do not choose the politicians, but on the contrary, that the latter are imposed on voters. By referring to political ideologies, the leadership of a party can impose on voters their political orientation and push them to elect candidates who do not deserve to be elected.'[4] As we will recall, this point exactly is made in Mosca: 'The truth is that the representative *has himself elected* by the voters.'[5] There is more than a hint of Michels when Jouvenel says: 'There is no need to suppose that the persons chosen to govern are not in general perfectly repre-

ford University Press, 1966), p. 190.

3   Slevin, 'Social Change and Human Values', pp. 51–2.

4   Gabriele Ciampini, 'The Elitism of Bertrand de Jouvenel: A Reinterpretation of Jouvenel's Political Theory Through the Elite Theory', *Academic Journal of Interdisciplinary Studies*, 2:21 (October 2013), p. 20.

5   Gaetano Mosca, *The Ruling Class*, ed. Arthur Livingston, trans. Hannah D. Khan (1895; New York: McGraw-Hill, 1939), p. 154.

sentative men, exactly resembling their subjects. But when
once they have been summoned to exercise of sovereign
authority, their wills take on [...] a new character and different force.'[6] While it is not clear if he ever read them, I
am confident in asserting that Jouvenel had instinctively
absorbed the core tenets of elite theory: Mosca's Law of
the Rulers and the Ruled, Pareto's Circulation of Elites,
and Michels's Iron Law of Oligarchy.[7]

Jouvenel's critique of democracy is rooted in two facts:
first, he says that Montesquieu's separation of powers is a
myth. 'Jouvenel argues that the principle of separation of
powers is actually unrealised. The Government should be
autonomous from the Parliament if it wants to enjoy any
substantial autonomy. The executive, which should be an
expression of the popular will, is in fact directed by parties'
leaders supporting it in Parliament.'[8] Second, he says that
'democratic political systems are not immune to the secular trend in the growth of central governmental power; in
fact, de Jouvenel argues, they provide the broadest high-
way to tyranny that has ever existed.'[9] On this score, he
laments the French Revolution: 'The Power of the people
was but a fiction in a regime which was for practical purposes a parliamentary sovereignty. But the fiction justified
the blotting out of liberty on a scale never known before in
Europe.'[10] His critique is virtually identical with that that

6   Bertrand de Jouvenel, *On Power: The Natural History of Its
Growth*, trans. J.F. Huntington (1945; Minneapolis, MN: Liberty
Fund, 1993), pp. 124–5.

7   See also Gabriele Ciampini, 'Is Bertrand de Jouvenel only a
Liberal Philosopher? The Relations between His Political Thought
with the Twentieth Century Sociological Thought', *International
Journal of Social Science and Humanity*, 3:5 (September 2013), pp.
448–52.

8   Gabriele Ciampini, 'The Elitism of Bertrand de Jouvenel', p. 21.

9   Pierce, *Contemporary French Political Thought*, p. 188.

10   Jouvenel, *On Power*, p. 322.

found in J. L. Talmon:

> The real people, or rather their leadership, once tri-
> umphant in their insurrection, become Rousseau's
> Legislator, who surveys clearly the whole panorama,
> without being swayed by partial interests and pas-
> sions, and shapes the "young nation" with the help
> of laws derived from his superior wisdom. He pre-
> pares it to will the general will. First comes the elim-
> ination of men and influences not of the people and
> not identified with the general will embodied in the
> newly established Social Contract of the Revolution;
> then the re-education of the young nation to will the
> general will.'[11]

Note here that the structure of power conforms exactly to
Schmitt's model: who decides? Who interprets? And, like
Schmitt, Jouvenel did not see democracy itself as different *in
formal terms* from any previous power structures.

Before outlining Jouvenel's famous high-low middle
mechanism, it is worth noting that he always maintained
that he was a kind of liberal, insomuch as he was concerned throughout his work with liberty and the limiting
of tyrannical power. At one point, in On Power, for example, he defends the traditional small-business-owning
bourgeois against centralising Power and its strategic use
of inflation to drain the savings of the middle classes: 'Tyr-
annies made their appearance in step with the inflation
which destroyed the independence and security of middle-class liberalism.'[12] However, he was also a severe critic of liberalism. In certain of his other works, which have
not been translated into English, 'he condemns his gener-
ation (including himself) for its simplistic view of man as
an individualistic and materialistic consumer, who can be

---

11   J. L. Talmon, *The Origins of Totalitarian Democracy* (London:
Secker and Warburg, 1952), p. 49.
12   Jouvenel, *On Power*, p. 385.

made completely happy by rationalization of the economic system, and the prevention of further wars.'13 As Carl Slevin tells us, Jouvenel was acutely aware of the problem of corporatocracy and liberalism's tendency to facilitate it:

> Liberalism, in its degenerate and anarchic form involving periodic crises and unemployment as in the U.S.A., implies even greater subjection of the individual to economic forces than does Communism. In addition, Liberalism is no longer efficient in satisfying consumer demands through competition, for out of the struggle to survive have emerged gigantic corporations and trusts, which can effectively distort the market for their own ends. In opposition to the fundamental tenets of Liberalism, enterprises threatened by the periodic depressions have called on the State for assistance, with great success, thereby making the consumer, in his guise as tax-payer, subsidize a system which offers no benefits in return.[14]

We will return to Jouvenel's view of capitalism and its relationship to power shortly, but for now it is enough to say that although he was very far from being a doctrinaire free-market libertarian, he maintained that the scope for liberty rested in the middle class, people of independent means, who did not have to rely on the state. He had this in common with Samuel T. Francis, whom we will consider later.

Let us turn now to outline Jouvenel's model. As I have said, it is often called the high-low middle mechanism and sometimes the patron theory of power. The idea at its most basic is that the high—the central power—makes an appeal of liberation and guarantee of security to the low who are being 'oppressed' by the middle. By patronising the low, the high thus starts to drain away the power of the middle, thus accruing more power to itself. The clearest explication of this model is not found in *On Power*, where it

13   Slevin, 'Social Change and Human Values', p. 58.
14   Slevin, 'Social Change and Human Values', p. 55.

emerges as a pattern throughout many historical episodes that the book considers, but in C. A. Bond's *Nemesis*, which does much to strip the model down to its core elements. Jouvenel tends to use the terms 'Power', 'aristocracy' and 'the common people' to define his three categories.[15] However, the situation is somewhat more complicated than this, since he also seems to treat the independent middle class as being separate from the aristocracy with whom it might ally should Power become tyrannical.[16] Bond prefers to use the terms: 'centre', 'subsidiary', and 'periphery'.[17] For this last group, 'periphery', Curtis Yarvin prefers 'clients': 'Marx's proletariat and lumpenproletariat, uneducated and/or dependent.'[18] I think 'clients' is a useful way to visualise the relationship of patronage between the high and the low; however, Bond's 'periphery' captures something of the passive helplessness of the low: 'without this alliance between a power centre and the periphery, the periphery itself is basically irrelevant.'[19]

While the high and low categories can be easily understood—the high is the central sovereign power, the low are the lowest strata of the great mass of people—the middle requires further elaboration. Here there are some complications and nuances that are not readily understood. We cannot confuse 'the middle' simply with the middle class. While Yarvin's term 'clients' is useful to think about the low, his use of the term 'commoners'—borrowed from Orwell—will not do for the middle. Jouvenel consistently

15   Jouvenel, *On Power*, p. 173.
16   Jouvenel, *On Power*, p. 384.
17   C. A. Bond, *Nemesis: The Jouvenelian vs. The Liberal Model of Human Orders* (Perth: Imperium Press, 2019), p. 4.
18   Curtis Yarvin, 'The Clear Pill, Part 1 of 5: The Four-Stroke Regime', The American Mind (27 September 2019): https://americanmind.org/salvo/the-clear-pill-part-1-of-5-the-four-stroke-regime/.
19   Bond, *Nemesis*, p, 6.

writes about the middle as an *aristocracy* which has its own centres of power or 'castles'. Bond describes 'subsidiaries' as follows:

> These subsidiary centres can be seen as delegates of the centre, and act in its name and under its authority. Jouvenel termed the elements that comprise this category 'social authorities', and by this he meant such entities as the nobility, families, corporations, trade unions, and any other institution within an order which can demand the obedience and allegiance of those within that order in conjunction with the central governing apparatus, or Power.[20]

The key point to grasp is that to count as 'aristocratic' or 'subsidiary', Power must perceive a cell as a *rival*. Jouvenel describes Power as having an almost psychotic need to snuff out any challenge to its monopoly of control. This is the 'inner essence of Power, which is the inevitable assailant of the social authorities and sucks their very lifeblood. And the more vigorous a particular Power is, the more virile it is in the role of vampire.' Power has a 'jealousy of any and every command, however small, which was not its own, Power could not tolerate such independence.'[21] For Jouvenel this is a *constant fact* of human history and can be observed from the earliest tribal cultures right through to the present. He discusses variously 'the clan cell', 'the baronial cell', and 'the capitalistic cell' which divides into the 'the industrial cell' and 'the financial cell'. But no matter the period and specifics of the case, the structure remains the same: Power seeks to destroy the rival powers in the subsidiaries by patronising clients. 'Power is the great leveller that sets out to curtail or eliminate every social authority that mediates between the individual and the state.'[22]

20   Bond, *Nemesis*, p. 4.
21   Jouvenel, *On Power*, pp. 176, 185.
22   Daniel J. Mahoney, *Bertrand de Jouvenel* (Wilmington, DE: ISI Books, 2005), p. 31.

However, there are two groups that Jouvenel discusses that are missing in this tripartite model: the middle class in general, and a group we might call *newly elevated bureaucrats*. I am afraid that here I will have to introduce some complexity by mapping Jouvenel's model onto the categories inherited from Mosca and Pareto: the governing-elite, the non-governing elite and the governed. The middle class *in general*, who include people that are independently wealthy enough not to need the state but who do not command power sufficient to be an aristocrat, form the upper part of the governed. We might call this class 'petite bourgeois' or we might call them 'kulaks'. They can ally with Power, or they can ally with the subsidiaries; should they ally with the latter, they too will become the target of Power which will brook no dissent. The *newly elevated bureaucrats*, meanwhile, become the lower stratum of the ruling class as non-governing elites. Let us take an example from Jouvenel:

> The natural requirements of Power made the fortunes of the common people. All those 'little people' whom Dupont-Ferrier shows us staffing the Treasure Court and the Taxes Court, no sooner found their niche in the state than they set about advancing their own fortunes along with their employers. At whose expense? The aristocrats'. With a boldness born of obscurity they encroached progressively on the taxing rights of the barons and transferred to the royal treasury the incomes of the great. As their invasions grew, the financial machine grew larger and more complicated. There might be new posts for their relations, they discovered new duties, so that whole families take their ease in a bureaucracy that grew continually in numbers and authority. [...] spawning [...] a whole hierarchy of underlings—deputies, clerks, registrars. So it was that everywhere the service of the state became the road to distinction, advancement, and authority for the common people. [...] What a sight it

is, the rise of the clerks, this swarming of busy bees who gradually devour the feudal splendour and leave it with nothing but its pomp and titles! Does it not leap to the eye that the state has made the fortunes of all these common people, just as they have made the state's?[23]

Jouvenel shared with Michels, it seems, an absolute distaste for the career bureaucrat. It is important to note, however, that these bureaucrats are *not* the low or peripheries or clients—they are a key part of Power itself on its march towards ever greater centralisation. Should any of the institutions of these bureaucrats begin to develop power *independently* from the central Power, then they become aristocrats, feudal nodes, who will in time draw the Eye of Sauron.

Let us examine a few of Jouvenel's historical examples that showcase his model in action:

> So in England, when the greed of Henry VIII had fallen on the ecclesiastical authorities to get from their wealth the wherewithal to carry out his policies the greater part of the monastic spoils stuck to the fingers of hands which had been held out to receive them. These spoils founded the fortunes of the nascent English capitalism. In this way new hives are forever being built, in which lie a new sort of energies; these will in time inspire the state of fresh orgies of covetousness.'[24]

Here Power—as vested in the king, Henry VIII, who let us not forget, was aided by skilled administrators such as Thomas Cromwell—crushes a subsidiary power, the Catholic church, as a simple raid on its wealth. But in the process, he could not help but raise up a new group of people who would themselves later become aristocrats. This is why Jouvenel described the state as a 'permanent revolution' since Power's ceaseless quest to eliminate its rivals invariably must create

23   Jouvenel, *On Power*, pp. 201–2.
24   Jouvenel, *On Power*, p. 177.

new potential rivals in the process.

Jouvenel later considers the same pattern taking place after the industrial revolution. The industrialists had become powerful by the end of the nineteenth century, and thus represented a *feudal threat* to Power, which had to respond by stripping it of that power either by co-opting it or else outright seizure of assets. He maintains that this has nothing whatsoever to do with ideology but is a pure function of power:

> In the end, calling it socialization or nationalization, the state strives to make its own all the great castles of the economic feudal system, the railway companies, the electricity distributing companies, and so on. Only those who know nothing of any time but their own, who are completely in the dark as to the manner of Power's behaving through thousands of years, would regard these proceedings as the fruit of a particular set of doctrines. They are in fact the normal manifestations of Power, and differ not at all in their nature from Henry VIII's confiscation of the wealth of the monasteries. The same principle is at work; the hunger for authority, the thirst for authorities; and in all these operations the same characteristics are present, including the rapid elevation of the dividers of the spoils. Whether it is socialist or whether it is not, Power must always be at war with the capitalist authorities and despoil the capitalists of their accumulated wealth: in doing so it obeys the law of nature.[25]

Jouvenel did not only have in mind the USSR or Nazi Germany, but also the USA from Theodore Roosevelt to Franklin D. Roosevelt, capitalists had to be *tamed and disciplined* by Power. By the end of World War II, it had been almost entirely successful in this, but at a cost: by heavily regulating hitherto private companies, Power had created massive corporations which were, as Bond emphasises, to-

25   Jouvenel, *On Power*, p. 186.

tal creations of the law, entirely dependent on the state for their existence.[26] Jouvenel called this state of affairs, 'syndicalist feudalism' which had grown to such 'Gargantuan proportions' that it presented Power with a problem:

> Will political Power, after beating capitalist feudalism with the help of syndicalist feudalism, now round on its ally? If it does not, it will be the syndicalist feudalisms, and not itself, which will exercise the vast powers committed to it by individuals. And the state then will be the 'public thing' of the syndicalist feudalisms.[27]

It seems to me that this has come to pass. At the time of writing, when Joe Biden is the President of the USA, it strikes me that he is the 'public thing' of much larger entities that have effective Power. 'Syndicalist feudalisms' have in many respects not only merged with the state but also usurped it as the central node of authority. The Investment firms Blackrock and Vanguard have over $9 trillion and $7 trillion in assets respectively. The most well-known corporate brand leaders typically enjoy over 70% market share in their specialist product lines with the second biggest brand taking the bulk of the rest of the pie creating effective duopolies in many markets. These corporate machines in turn fund massive and extremely influential non-government organizations (NGOs) and lobby groups as well as exercising a near-total dominance of the media. It is quite clear that democratic political leaders are today merely showmen and that effective sovereignty, in Schmitt's terms, lies in the syndicalist nexus. Since the Power has become unmistakably corporate and globalist, unmoored from any national state, it becomes ravenous in its search for independent rival powers and demands obedience becoming distinctly totalitarian.

At the time of writing, we have been suffering the COVID-19 pandemic for almost two years. Scarcely any

26   Bond, *Nemesis*, pp. 88–100.
27   Jouvenel, *On Power*, p. 187.

media organisations will speak out against harsh governmental restrictions; the media does the bidding of Power without question. Corporations walk in lockstep carrying the same message, actively censoring countervailing voices. We are experiencing the greatest wealth transfer from the middle class to elites in history.[28] From the start of the pandemic to April 2021, Amazon's profits increased by 220% as many small and medium firms closed and the public experienced record inflation.[29] The failure of Power to check syndicalist feudalisms has come to pass and now the tail wags the dog:

> Where will it end? In the destruction of all other command for the benefit of one alone—that of the state. In each man's absolute freedom from every family and social authority, a freedom the price of which is complete submission to the state. In the complete equality as between themselves of all citizens, paid for by their equal abasement before the power of their absolute master—the state. In the disappearance of every constraint which does not emanate from the state, and in the denial of every pre-eminence which is not approved by the state. In a word, it ends in the atomization of society, and in the rupture of every private tie linking man and man, whose only bond is now their common bondage to the state. The extremes of individualism and socialism meet: that was their predestined course.'[30]

28   Carol Roth, 'The Greatest Transfer of Wealth From the Middle Class to the Elites in History', Brownstone Institute (1 November 2021): https://brownstone.org/articles/the-greatest-transfer-of-wealth-from-the-middle-class-to-the-elites-in-history/.
29   Karen Weise, 'Amazon's Profit Soars 220 Percent as Pandemic Drives Shopping Online', New York Times (29 April 2021): https://www.nytimes.com/2021/04/29/technology/amazons-profits-triple.html.
30   Jouvenel, *On Power*, p. 187.

If we are not there yet, it certainly feels that way. Historically if Power is seen as rotten to the core, revolution beckons.

Jouvenel devotes an entire chapter to revolutions. He argues that historians typically misunderstand revolutions because they are violent and therefore treated as in some way exceptional. He maintains, however, that revolutions too conform to his model. He remarks on the fact that most revolutions result in a system with a stronger central power than before:

> Before the rapids, there was a rule of a Charles I, a Louis XVI, a Nicholas II. After them, that of a Cromwell, a Napoleon, a Stalin. [...] The Cromwells and Stalins are no fortuitous consequence, no accidental happening, of the revolutionary tempest. Rather they are its predestined goal, towards which the entire upheaval was moving inevitably; the cycle began with the downfall of an inadequate Power only to close with the consolidation of a more absolute Power.[31]

For Jouvenel, revolution is the consequence of a weakness in Power which is liquidated by a stronger one. The incumbent Power will be 'weary and sceptical', 'worn out, inspiring modest respect, and with no more than a faded authority left to it'—what Jouvenel calls a 'nerveless scarecrow'.[32] How does a revolution happen? It is typically—and this has more than an echo of Pareto's foxes and lions about it—a refusal to use force on the part of Power.

> Did the people rise against Louis XIV? No, but against the good-natured Louis XVI, who had not even the nerve to let his Swiss Guards open fire. Against Peter the Great? No, but against the weakling Nicolas II, who did not dare avenge his beloved Rasputin. Against the old bluebeard, Henry VIII? No, but against Charles I, who, after a few fitful attempts

31   Jouvenel, *On Power*, p. 238.
32   Jouvenel, *On Power*, p. 241.

at governing, had resigned himself to living in a small way and was no danger to anyone.[33]

The moment of truth for any regime will come at the moment in which ideological 'soft power' is stripped away and it must use repressive force to crush its opposition. Hesitancy on the part of Power at the hour of decision—whether through a failure of nerve in the leadership or a failure in confidence on the part of their generals—will seal their fate if rival aristocrats exploit popular discontent.

What is the benefit of reading Jouvenel? What can he give us that we cannot find in the elite theorists or in Schmitt? I believe he gives us a dynamic model of *change* that is somewhat taken for granted in the other thinkers. Mosca discusses the tendency towards feudalism or towards bureaucratisation but does not explain *how* a society transitions from one state to the next, or indeed, *why*; Jouvenel does. Pareto outlines his circulation of elites, and the predominance of foxes or lions in the ruling class, but he does not give us the *exact mechanism* through which this happens; Jouvenel does. Schmitt states that every sovereign must declare its friends and enemies, but Jouvenel provides a *rationale* for who might be the sovereign's enemy at any given point. For example, in 2021, the US Federal Government—the public face of the aforementioned syndicalist nexus of finance, corporations, and NGOs—has declared that 'white supremacists' constitute the highest terrorist threat to the country; former President George W. Bush even argued they belong in the same breath as ISIS and that, in a statement as Schmittian as any ever uttered, 'bigotry and white supremacy are "blasphemy" against the American creed.'[34] The media daily propagandises against

---

33   Jouvenel, *On Power*, p. 240.
34   Maegan Vazquez, 'George W. Bush: Bigotry and White Supremacy are "Blasphemy" against the American Creed' (19 October 2017):   https://edition.cnn.com/2017/10/19/politics/bush-free-

'white privilege', explains why white people are 'the problem'. But why would Power focus so heavily on this group, 'white people'? It is because it comprises people who are independent of the state, would-be aristocrats, subsidiaries *in potential*, and even a few truly independent institutions, and therefore represents the largest threat to its hegemony. This was embodied in the hated figure of Donald Trump, but since he was banished from the airwaves and social media, now it must take the form of a direct attack on the disobedient people themselves, *especially* if they have refused the vaccination against the pandemic which is a very convenient proxy marker of 'friend' or 'enemy' to Power. Jouvenel as a guide would tell us two things: first, one way or the other, the hour of decision will come; second, whatever order exists after this hour of decision will grant no more 'liberty' than what came before—the game stays the same, only the players change.

dom-event/index.html.

Chapter 7
MANAGERIAL ELITES

In the 1930s, James Burnham had been one of the leading American exponents of Trotskyism. However, in the 1940s, he broke decisively with Marxism and 'accepted the basic validity' of the Italian elite theorists (Mosca, Pareto and Michels) to whom he had been introduced by Sidney Hook.[1] In 1941, he published his most famous book, *The Managerial Revolution*, which argued that Marxism had misconceived the true nature of the revolution that had taken place—it was not the proletariat who overthrew bourgeois capitalism but a new class, the managerial class. This book created an intellectual storm at the time of its publication and was reviewed very widely, not only by academic journals but also by mainstream newspapers. Two years later, he followed it up with *The Machiavellians* in which he explored the ideas of the elite theorists together with Georges Sorel and from which I have already drawn. Burnham was read by and profoundly influenced George Orwell, who was chilled by his amoral scientific view of power.[2] Burnham's outline of the managerial state inspired both *Animal Farm* and *1984*; his coldly realist view was said to be the model for the both the character O'Brien

1   Sidney Hook, 'On James Burnham's The Machiavellians', *Society*, 25 (March 1988), p. 68.
2   See George Orwell, 'James Burnham and the Managerial Revolution' and 'Review of The Machiavellians by James Burnham' in *Essays* (New York: Everyman's Library, 2002), pp. 523–6, 1052–73.

and the book, *The Theory and Practice of Oligarchical Collectivism*, by Emmanuel Goldstein in the latter.[3] In the 1950s and beyond, he became part of the conservative establishment in the USA, helping William F. Buckley found *National Review* and becoming a leading advocate of a tough line against the Soviet Union during the Cold War—to the extent that now Burnham is sometimes called 'the first Neoconservative'.[4] Later, in 1964, he published *The Suicide of the West*, in which he is severely critical of liberal attitudes and assumptions which he argued are naïve to the point of being suicidal.[5]

Here we will focus on the core ideas of *The Managerial Revolution* rather than the entire body of his thought.[6] It is obvious to anyone familiar with the elite theorists that Burnham had fully internalised the teachings of Mosca, Pareto, and Michels. So as not to repeat ourselves, we will take their conclusions as granted, and suffice only to show what is original in Burnham. In 1960, Burnham wrote a short article called 'Managing the Managers', which condensed his core thesis to just five pages.[7] This very useful summary will serve as a guideline throughout.

Before starting, it is important to emphasise Burnham's explicitly Machiavellian frame. 'There is little optimism in

---

3   R. B. Reaves, 'Orwell's "Second Thoughts on James Burnham" and 1984', *College Literature*, 11:1 (1984), pp. 13–21.

4   Binoy Kampmark, 'The First Neo-conservative: James Burnham and the Origins of a Movement', *Review of International Studies*, 37:4 (2011), pp. 1885–1907.

5   James Burnham, *Suicide of the West: An Essay on the Meaning and Destiny of Liberalism* (New York: John Day Company, 1964).

6   For a very good overview see Daniel J. O'Neil, 'The Political Philosophy of James Burnham', *International Journal of Social Economics*, 21 (1994), pp. 141–52; for a book-length treatment see Samuel T. Francis, Thinkers of our Time: James Burnham (1984; London: The Claridge Press, 1999).

7   James Burnham, 'Managing the Managers', *Challenge*, 8:8 (May 1960), pp. 18–23.

Burnham's view of human nature.'[8] Of all the thinkers we are considering, he was the one who most emphatically and avowedly wore the mantle of 'Machiavellian'—seeking to write only about what is, not what ought to be. He embodied what Thomas Sowell might call the 'constrained' or 'tragic' vision of man.[9] Niccolò Machiavelli once said that 'human appetites are insatiable',[10] but the thing that they desire most is not wealth but power. Burnham's fundamental view of human nature was a Hobbesian struggle driven by an almost Nietzschean Will to Power. Perhaps this is nowhere more evident than in *Suicide of the West* when he argues that the liberal assumption that mass education would solve the problems of yesteryear is wrong-headed: 'The nineteenth-century liberals overlooked, and the twentieth-century liberals decline to face, the fact that teaching everyone to read opens minds to propaganda and indoctrination at least as much as to truths.'[11] No one truly strives for the 'public good' but rather to seeks to increase 'power and prestige for himself and his clique'.[12] 'Burnham thus harboured no illusion that a particular form of society—agrarian, theocratic, or feudal, much less socialist, liberal, or democratic—could adequately restrain the appetite for power.'[13] Like Mosca, he recognised the need and utility of a 'political formula' which can apparently motivate men by appealing to their sentiments, but like Pareto, he

8   O'Neil, 'The Political Philosophy of James Burnham', p. 143.
9   Thomas Sowell, *A Conflict of Visions: Ideological Origins of Political Struggles*, rev. ed. (1987; New York: Basic Books, 2007), p. 162.
10   Niccolò Machiavelli, *Discourses on Livy*, trans. Harvey C. Mansfield and Nathan Tarcov (1517; Chicago: University of Chicago Press, 1996), 2. Preface, p. 125.
11   Burnham, *Suicide of the West*, pp. 138–9.
12   O'Neil, 'The Political Philosophy of James Burnham', p. 143.
13   Samuel T. Francis, 'The Other Side of Modernism: James Burnham and His Legacy', in *Beautiful Losers* (Columbia, MI: University of Missouri Press, 1994), p. 133.

essentially viewed all ideologies as thinly-veiled justifications for the interests of power. However, unlike Pareto,
who saw psychology as the decisive factor, Burnham retained—perhaps from his Marxist origins—an economic
emphasis as we shall see.

Where the analysis of power and the ruling class has
conventionally rested in the government itself, Burnham
saw the managerial class operating across the so-called
public-private divide and in every large organisation. In
effect, the bureaucrats who emerge in Mosca and Michels,
through the iron law of oligarchy, come to control every
institution and then come to recognise each other as an
identifiable class with common skills, interests, beliefs,
and goals.

> In the new form of society, sovereignty is localized
> in administrative bureaus. They proclaim the rules,
> make the laws, issue the decrees. The shift from par-
> liament to the bureaus occurs on a world scale [...]
> The actual directing and administrative work of the
> bureaus is carried on by new men, a new type of men.
> It is, specifically, the *managerial* type [...] The active
> heads of the bureaus are the managers-in-govern-
> ment, the same, or nearly the same, in training, func-
> tions, skills, habits of thought as the managers-in-in-
> dustry.[14]

Thus, power seems as if it is decentralising but, in fact, is
concentrating and consolidating itself in a more diffuse way
across every possible institutional node in society. If we use
Jouvenel's idea of power centres being like castles which central power needs to capture, the managerial class quietly takes
over government while capturing every castle to create an
extremely broad 'central' power base which has the appearance of being made up of disparate and separate spheres of

---

14   James Burnham, *The Managerial Revolution* (1941; Westport,
CN: Greenwood Press, 1972), pp. 148–50.

influence.

When Burnham talks about 'managers-in-industry' and 'managers-in-government', it brings to mind the corporate middle manager and the career civil servant, but he actually has in mind a much wider range of people than that. Senior executives at board level in corporations, for example—the CEO—are very often 'managers', paid employees. Beyond the mid-ranking civil servants, top-level advisors of every stripe, senior diplomats, communications directors and so on are all 'managers'. Even the politicians themselves who sit in Parliamentary democracies—we might picture someone like Tony Blair or Angela Merkel—take on a distinctly managerial air. However, the scope of the managerial class is wider still than this: it is not simply those who work in and around corporations and governments, but in *all* major institutions across society. It is worth quoting Burnham at length here:

> Within the huge trade unions, a similar managerial officialdom, the 'labor bureaucracy,' consolidates its position as an elite. This elite is sharply distinguished in training, income, habits and outlook from the ordinary union member. The trend extends to the military world, the academic world, the non-profit foundations and even auxiliary organizations of the U.N. Armies are no longer run by 'fighting captains,' but by a Pentagon-style managerial bureaucracy. Within the universities, proliferating administrators have risen above students, teaching faculty, alumni and parents, their power position expressed in the symbols of higher salaries and special privileges. The great 'nonprofit foundations' have been transformed from expressions of individual benevolence into strategic bases of managerial-administrative power. The United Nations has an international echelon of managers entrenched in the Secretariat. There are fairly obvious parallels in the managerial structures of the diverse institutional fields. For example, managers in

> business are to stockholders as labor managers are to
> union members; as government managers are to vot-
> ers; as public school administrators are to tax-payers;
> as university and private school administrators are to
> tuition payers and fund contributors.[15]

When Burnham was writing, the managerial class had not
fully consolidated its power so the truth of what he was saying was not readily visible to all but the most astute observ-
ers. Detractors would often focus on irrelevant details and
incorrect predictions while missing the bigger picture.[16] At
the time of writing, in the 2020s, when all these organisations appear to speak with one voice, when none dare to dis-
agree, the truth of Burnham's analysis appears so obvious as
to seem trite. In fact, the scope now extends beyond what
even he envisioned to encompass practically every major
Church denomination too.

Where Marxists believed that the decisive factor in history and society is ownership of the means of production,
Burnham argued that the relationship between ownership
and control had been severed due to the rise of limited li-
ability corporations—which, as C. A. Bond shows, were
always a legal creation rather than a facet of the free market[17]—as well as the fact of mass and scale.

> The divorce of control, or power, from ownership
> has been due in large part to the growth of public cor-
> porations. So long as a single person, family or com-
> paratively small group held a substantial portion of
> the common shares of a corporation, the legal 'own-
> ers' could control its affairs. Even if they no longer ac-
> tually conducted the business, the operating manag-
> ers were functioning as their accountable agents. But
> when the enterprise became more vast in scope and,

15   Burnham, 'Managing the Managers', p. 19.
16   See Francis, *Thinkers of Our Time*, pp. 26–8.
17   C. A. Bond, *Nemesis: The Jouvenelian vs. The Liberal Model of
Human Orders* (Perth: Imperium Press, 2019), pp. 88–101.

at the same time, the stock certificates became spread in small bundles among thousands of persons, the managers were gradually released from subordination to the nominal owners. *De facto* control passed, for the most part, to nonowning management.[18]

In effect, Burnham's key insight was to apply Michels's iron law of oligarchy to shareholders and corporate managers and then to apply the same logic to every other organisation across society.

Burnham's conception of the behaviour and methods of managerial elites owes a lot to Michels. They look after their own interests at the expense of those whom they are supposed to represent and serve:

> Once the managers consolidate their position within an institution, their objective interests no longer fully correspond to the interests of the other groups involved—voters, owners, members, teachers, students or consumers. A decision on dividends, mergers, labor contracts, prices, curriculum, class size, scope of government operations, armament, strikes, etc., may serve the best interests of the managers without necessarily contributing to the well-being of the other groups.[19]

Their ends are almost entirely self-serving and self-justifying, focusing on 'problems' that expand their control and power:

> Managerial activity tends to become inbred and self-justifying. The enterprise comes to be thought of as existing for the sake of its managers—not the managers for the enterprise. A high percentage of the time of the managers and their staff is spent on 'housekeeping' and other internal problems. [...] Self-justifying managerial control tends to keep alive

18   Burnham, 'Managing the Managers', p. 18.
19   Burnham, 'Managing the Managers', p. 20.

operations which have little social purpose other than to nourish an enclave of managers. This is conspicuously true of governments. Many acute, expensive problems which our society faces—for example, in agriculture, radio-TV, railroads, finance, etc.—are largely manufactured by the managerial agencies founded to solve them.[20]

Here one might think of the issue of climate change or the response to the COVID-19 pandemic; in both cases every 'solution' to the problem entails expanding the remit of the managers, creating new jobs for managers, and instituting new power centres from which managers can control the masses.

In addition, the managerial class is anti-democratic in practice though not in rhetoric:

Managerial predominance tends toward regimentation and the suppression of active democracy. The rising power of a managerial group in a given institution is, in fact, usually equivalent to a lessening in whatever form of democracy is relevant. In other words, the power of the stockholder, voter, member, consumer, faculty, taxpayer, etc., decreases as the power of the manager increases. The combination of managerial groups—as when there is collusion between labor and business management—means the decline of democracy in the conjoined fields. In this connection, we must remember that totalitarianism is nothing more than an integrated front of managerial groups achieved either by mutual agreement or unilateral coercion.[21]

They are also practically impossible to dispense with owing to the interchangeable nature of managers:

Even today, though individual managers in business can lose their jobs, a Napoleonic campaign is needed

20 Burnham, 'Managing the Managers', p. 21.
21 Burnham, 'Managing the Managers', p. 21.

to get rid of a corporate management group. As for government or educational administrators and trade union officials, a nuclear explosion would hardly be enough to dislodge them.[22]

Firing one manager will simply result in another one taking his place; he will have the same managerial tastes, interests, ideas, goals and so on as the last one.

Why did this change come about? For Burnham, it is no great secret:

> There is no mystery in this shift. It can be correlated easily enough with the change in character of the state's activities. Parliament was the sovereign body of the limited state of capitalism. The bureaus are the sovereign bodies of the unlimited state of managerial society.[23]

Indeed, much of *The Managerial Revolution* is devoted to contrasting 'capitalism', by which Burnham means the small-state laissez-faire bourgeois capitalism of nineteenth century, with managerialism. The differences between capitalism and managerialism manifest themselves in their respective ideologies. Capitalist societies promoted: '*individualism*; opportunity; "natural rights", especially the rights of property; freedom, especially "freedom of contract"; private enterprise; private initiative; and so on.' These ideas 'justified profit and interest', 'they showed why the owner of the instruments of production was entitled to the full product of those instruments and why the worker had no claim on the owner except for the contracted wages.'[24] Burnham notes that where these were once progressive slogans, in 1941 they are recognised as reactionary and as the cries of Tories. In contrast, managerialism is orientated away from the private individual and towards the public collective; away from free enterprise and

22   Burnham, 'Managing the Managers', p. 20.
23   Burnham, *The Managerial Revolution*, p. 148.
24   Burnham, *The Managerial Revolution*, p. 187.

towards planning; away from providing opportunities and towards providing jobs; less about 'rights' and more about 'duties'. One must remember here that Burnham did not only have the United States in mind but also the Soviet Union and Nazi Germany as managerial states. The Soviets and Germans were more blatant in their messaging than the Americans who felt the need to pay lip-service to the older ideologies. In a passage that seems shocking to read today—perhaps owing to the eighty years of propaganda between 1941 and now—Burnham notes that the masses in Britain, France, and America simply did not want to fight World War II for the elites—that their messaging was tired and outmoded, and simply failed to animate the young men *despite* mass unemployment at the time. He contrasts that with the picture in Germany, where the masses enthusiastically supported Hitler. He argues that it is 'shallow and absurd' to imagine that mass support for the German war effort was down to terrorism and skilled propaganda alone—rather, the cause was genuinely popular. In France, meanwhile, the masses were 'passive' and 'did not have the will to fight' because 'democracy' and 'capitalism' were not causes that animated them whatsoever. He points out the awkward and undeniable fact that both Britain and the USA had to resort to the draft rather than relying on millions of enthusiastic and willing volunteers *at a time of mass unemployment*.[25] However, managerialism ultimately has a globalising tendency and 'totalitarian character.'[26] As Burnham warned in 1960: 'the directing managers of each nation should preserve a healthy remnant of national individuality from becoming dissolved into the global managerial state that looms, under a variety of labels, as the ideal goal of a total managerial society.'[27]

However, it seems that Burnham's thinking retains a residually Marxist economism, whereby material conditions ultimately create the need for ideologies—or in Marxist

25   Burnham, *The Managerial Revolution*, pp. 189–90.
26   Francis, *Thinkers of Our Time*, p. 16.
27   Burnham, 'Managing the Managers', p.23.

jargon, the base creates the superstructure. The process by which capitalist firms 'become' managerial is driven initially by economic and practical concerns and only latterly by ideological ones. Burnham argues that managerialism comes about initially because of the economic need for start-up capital, especially in times of contraction in which interest rates are high, and investors are risk averse, such as during the Great Depression.

> [T]he internal crisis of entrepreneurial capitalism compels the expansion of the state. Massive amounts of new capital cannot be mobilised from private sources and must come, directly or indirectly, from the government. The managers indispensable to the technical processes of modern production, find co-operation with the state and the use of its coercive monopoly valuable for the continuance of production and for their own interests.[28]

Here, the defender of entrepreneurial capitalism might object and argue that a firm might raise funds by floating themselves on the stock market as an IPO—in other words, issuing shares in exchange for liquid capital. But the publicly traded company relies on the state for its legal status and automatically comes under increased regulation and managerial oversight. Furthermore, in practical terms, *control* over such companies is often handed over to managers.

For example, one of the great American tycoons, Henry Ford, died in 1947. Although his son Edsel had technically been the President of the Ford Motor Company from 1919 until his death in 1943, Henry had always assumed *de facto* control over the company; the board and the management had never seriously defied him. The Roosevelt administration had developed a plan to nationalise the Ford Motor Company should Henry become incapacitated—thus he resumed direct control of the firm. Before his death, ow-

28 Francis, *Thinkers of Our Time*, p. 14.

ing to his old age and declining mental health, and somewhat cajoled by his wife and daughter-in-law who owned controlling stakes in the firm, he agreed to hand over the day-to-day affairs of running the Ford Motor Company to his grandson Henry Ford II. It was soon losing $9 million a month and the corporate manager, Ernest R. Breech, was hired to become Executive Vice President and then Board Chairman. The Ford Motor Company became publicly traded in 1956.[29] Thus, even though the Ford family retain a 40% ownership of this company, it can be said to have fully transitioned into being a node of *managerialism* after the death of its founder, Henry Ford, who once commanded it as a visionary entrepreneur and leader.

The same can be said, and doubly so, for the Ford Foundation. Shortly after Henry Ford's death, Henry Ford II signed a document stating that the Ford family would exercise no more influence over the foundation than any other board member; he regretted the decision for the rest of his life. Since then, the Ford Foundation has supported almost exclusively left-wing progressive causes that would make Henry Ford—a well-known social conservative—turn in his grave.[30] For example, between 1970 and 2010, the Ford Foundation gave $46,123,135 to LGBT causes alone.[31] This is typical of how managerialism captures institutions and turns them against their original purposes for managerial ones. Here 'left-wing progressivism' and 'managerialism' are synonymous since the solutions of the former always involve the expansion of the latter. To stay with the example of LGBT causes, these may seem remote from

29   Charles E. Sorensen, *My Forty Years with Ford* (New York: Norton, 1956), pp. 324–33.
30   Martin Morse Wooster, *The Great Philanthropists and the Problem of 'Donor Intent'*, 3rd edn (1998; Washington, DC: Capital Research Center, 2007), pp. 34–44.
31   Scott Howard, *The Transgender Industrial Complex* (Quakertown, PA: Antelope Hill, 2020), p. 121.

something as technical as 'managerialism', but consider the armies of HR officers, diversity tsars, equalities ministers, and so on that are supported today under the banner of 'LGBT' and used to police and control enterprises. The 'philanthropic' endeavours of the Ford Foundation in this regard laid the infrastructure and groundwork to setup new power centres for managerialism under the guise of this ostensibly unrelated cause. Similar case studies can be found in issues as diverse as racial equality, gender equality, Islamist terrorism, climate change, mental health, and the management of the COVID-19 pandemic. The *logic* of managerialism is to create invisible 'problems' which can, in effect, never truly be solved, but rather can permanently support managerial jobs that force some arbitrary compliance standard such as 'unconscious bias training', 'net zero carbon', the ratio of men and women on executive boards, or whatever else. In the managerial state of the Soviet Union, such managers would simply be called commissars of the CPSU; in the managerial state of the United States they will simply be called things like 'Equality, Diversity and Inclusion Officer for Ford Motor Company', but their function is identical. In both cases, their post and its duties are backed by the full force of the law and the state. The latter is an example of the 'fused political-economic apparatus' Burnham describes.[32] In the end, Franklin D. Roosevelt did not have to nationalise Ford: even if the US government and the Ford Motor Company have the ostensible appearance of being separate entities, in actuality they move as one, espouse the same values, enforce the same compliance policies, and so on as if they were two sub-departments of The Politburo.

Thus, we can see that although, to retain the Marxist lexicon, the 'economic base' determines the 'ideological superstructure' in Burnham, managerialism also uses the

32 Burnham, *The Managerial Revolution*, p. 123.

ideological superstructure—which is to say the slogans of 'social justice' or 'climate change' etc—to expand its economic base and therefore its control. The role of public relations in general is somewhat taken for granted in Burnham and reduced to 'propaganda', even though—as we saw earlier—he was acutely aware of the power of the press to brainwash the public. He was also aware that the United States had come to be dominated by Pareto's foxes who rely almost exclusively on persuasion to get their way. This aspect of managerialism takes a subordinate role in Burnham's work but is massively expanded upon in the work of Samuel T. Francis, which we will explore shortly.

While Burnham worked chiefly in the diagnostic mode, he makes some suggestions as to how Western society might escape managerial totalitarianism—in fact, this is the central thesis of his next book, *The Machiavellians*. Burnham had a 'belief in a pluralist society, in which power restrains power'.[33] Thus his solution to managerial totalitarianism was essentially to set managers from different spheres against each other as to prevent them from uniting: 'The only way to manage the managers, in short, is to keep them busy enough managing or counter-vailing each other to guarantee that they won't unite and spend all their time managing the rest of us.'[34] This is substantially the same 'solution' as Mosca's juridical defence and separation of powers. However, as Jouvenel's work shows historically, and as history since Burnham was writing has shown, this is easier said than done because power's logic always tends towards centralisation and, it seems to me, that the managers have a *vested interest* in convergence. At the time of writing, they have achieved total global dominance across all institutions. It strikes me that of the possible rival nodes of power only two have the potential to

33   Hook, *On James Burnham's The Machiavellians'*, p. 68.
34   Burnham, 'Managing the Managers', p.23.

resist this total dominance. The first are the kulak class or, if you prefer, the independent middle-class or petite bourgeoise, who are non-managerial, disparate and are not (as yet) organised as a minority interest group. The second are managers at the level of *national* government whose power represents a threat to global managerialism and therefore must, in the long run, be conquered and dissolved as so many feudal castles. So long as armies are loyal to nations rather than to global governance structures or supra-national organisations, there remains at least the foreseeable *chance* that a power struggle may emerge between the traditional apparatuses of nation-states and the power centres of globalism. At present, they are united, but if history tells us anything at all, it is that things can change quickly.

On this score, in *The Machiavellians*, one thing Burnham does add to the elite theorists is his own idea of how revolutions take place:

> There is revolutionary change (1) when the élite cannot or will not adjust to the new technological and social forces; (2) when a significant proportion of the élite rejects ruling for cultural and aesthetic activities; (3) when the élite fails to assimilate promising new elements; (4) when a sizeable percentage of the élite questions the legitimacy of its rule; (5) when élite and non-élite reject the mythological basis of order in the society; and finally (6) when the ruling class lacks courage to employ force effectively.[35]

It is notable that of these six criteria *only one* considers the discontent of the masses and, even then, it is only half of the point; or, in other words, five and a half out of six criteria concern the elites. When considering our current situation

---

35   O'Neil, 'The Political Philosophy of James Burnham', p. 145. See also James Burnham, *The Machiavellians: Defenders of Freedom* (London: Putnam, 1943), pp. 257–8.

under managerial dominance, we might say that the current elite do adjust to new technologies, still have an insatiable appetite to rule, do not question their own legitimacy and believe their own myths. So far, so good.

However, to go through the six points again, they are at risk of mismanaging new technologies if they are too forceful in their climate change agenda. People accustomed to driving their own cars and enjoying other methods of travel and who are used to eating meat at affordable prices are likely revolt should these luxuries be suddenly removed, and they may find some elite backing by vested interests who still want to make money from the massive industries associated with them. They have also not yet found a way to manage the 'new social forces' unleashed by widespread resentment against mass immigration and other facets of globalism that led to the Brexit vote in the UK, Donald Trump in the United States, and so-called populism in Europe, most recently embodied by the meteoric rise of Éric Zemmour in France who has flanked Marine Le Pen by being more radical in his rhetoric to challenge the widely disliked globalist Emmanuel Macron. The current tactic of simply branding such people as 'beyond the pale', 'insurrectionists', 'fascists' *ad nauseum* has not worked in any respect since 2015. In fact, four years of such relentless rhetoric from the corporate media resulted in the hated Donald Trump increasing his total votes by over 14 million people—which would have been a resounding victory had he not been against the most popular presidential candidate of all time, Joe Biden. The populist phenomena are perhaps a symptom of the fact that managerial dominance and convergence will increasingly seek to dissolve the nation state as an obsolete unit. Indeed, globalists use separatist groups such as the SNP in Scotland or the Catalan independence movement in Spain as battering rams against the national governments. In Jouvenelian terms, if globalists constitute the centre and separatists the peripheries, then national governments are the subsidiaries whose feudal castles must, in the long run, be destroyed. So long as national governments maintain standing armies, it is possible to imagine scenarios in which they may turn on the globalists. For example, if populations simply will not brook the punitive carbon taxes that globalists wish them to enact, the political incentives to side with dissidents against globalists may be too strong for leaders to resist.

The elite are also actively turning away 'promising new elements' which is simply to say talented people with the wrong political views, skin colour, or gender. Either these people are not hired in the first place because of affirmative action programmes and increasingly absurd diversity quotas, or they are hired but later sacked for transgressing the regime in some way. In the long run, this will create an entire class of disaffected would-be elites who will put their skills and talents towards their eventual overthrow, especially if they feel locked out of what would have been their career path in a normal and well-run society. Furthermore, around thirty percent of people have turned decisively against the elites in the past few years, taken together with disaffected would-be elite, these dissidents form a non-elite who increasingly 'reject the mythological basis of order in the society' where this basis is some empty managerial slogan of social justice that becomes a *precondition* to enter the workplace. Which brings us finally to the question of force and whether the managerial foxes are prepared to use it against the dissident population. Time will surely tell, but according to Burnham's criteria, while the managerial elite may look secure and united now, they are faced with a threat that cannot be 'managed' using their usual tricks of persuasion since the people who constitute that threat have become actively hostile to their increasingly patronising messaging. Force will become necessary, and then, as Oswald Spengler once put it, will come the hour of decision.[36]

36   Oswald Spengler, *The Hour of Decision: Germany and World-Historical Evolution* (1934; Honolulu, HI: University Press of the Pacific, 2002).

Chapter 8
ELITES AND IDEOLOGY

Samuel T. Francis appears to have written *Leviathan and Its Enemies* in 1991 because this is when he dated its preface. He did not publish it during his lifetime. He died in 2005 and it was found by Jerry Woodruff who was given 'a box of 3.5-inch computer "floppy disks"' one of which was 'labeled in Sam's handwriting, "Leviathan and Its Enemies Complete" [...] dated "3-27-95" and contain[ing] Word Perfect 5.1 text files'.[1] It was published in 2016. Francis had been a firebrand paleoconservative journalist who wrote regular syndicated columns as well as speeches for Pat Buchanan. He was an early victim of 'cancel culture' for his politically incorrect statements about race and was fired by the *Washington Times* after an attack by the neo-conservative Dinesh D'Souza.[2] He was known for his sharp analytical insights, blistering rhetorical

1   Jerry Woodruff, 'Introduction', in Samuel T. Francis, *Leviathan and Its Enemies* (Arlington, VA: Washington Summit Publishers, 2016), pp. xi–xii.
2   Howard Kurtz, 'Washington Times Clips Its Right Wing', The Washington Post (October, 1995): https://www.washingtonpost.com/archive/lifestyle/1995/10/19/washington-times-clips-its-right-wing/dd009c93-883b-446c-bbbf-94c0a0570a1a/.   A book-length collection on the tendency of neo-conservatives to 'cancel' voices to their right can be found in Paul E. Gottfried and Richard B. Spencer (eds), *The Great Purge* (Arlington, VA: Washington Summit Publishers, 2015).

style, and a barbed wit. Posthumously, he was blamed (or praised, depending on who was writing) as the intellectual basis for the rise of Donald Trump.[3] Whatever controversies surrounded him in life, intellectual history will record Francis as a much more important and influential thinker than D'Souza or any neoconservative writer for *The National Review*. However, *Leviathan and Its Enemies* features none of Francis's signature polemics and is written in a more coolly analytical mode.

Francis had long been a protégé of James Burnham having written a monograph on him in 1984 that was republished in 1999.[4] *Leviathan and Its Enemies* can largely be read as a 1990s update of *The Managerial Revolution*. Francis had fully internalised the thought of the elite theorists and of his mentor, and much of the book covers terrain that we have already traversed. Thus, what is of interest to us here is what Francis *adds* to Burnham or else where he disagrees with him.

One important dimension of *Leviathan and Its Enemies* is that it has the benefit of fifty years of hindsight since Burnham wrote *The Managerial Revolution* during which time many objections were raised against the managerial thesis. After restating Burnham's central arguments at some length, Francis devotes considerable space to dealing with the chief counterarguments that were raised since 1941. The foremost of these came from C. Wright Mills whose book *The Power Elite*, published in 1956, constituted the main left-wing rebuttal to Burnham.[5] The chief conten-

3   Rod Dreher, 'Nation First, Conservatism Second', The American Conservative (19 January 2016): https://www.theamerican-conservative.com/dreher/nationalism-conservatism-trump-samuel-francis/.
4   Samuel T. Francis, *Thinkers of our Time: James Burnham* (1984; London: The Claridge Press, 1999).
5   C. Wright Mills, *The Power Elite* (1956; Oxford: Oxford University Press, 2000).

tion was that although the managerial function undoubtedly exists, propertied elites maintain a controlling ownership over firms. For example, when I discussed Burnham,
I used the example of the Ford Motor Company of a firm
transitioning from the entrepreneurial to the managerial. However, as I noted, the Ford family maintains to this
day a 40% stake in the company. In addition, William Clay
Ford Jr., the great-grandson of the founder, currently
serves as Executive Chairman having previously acted as
President, CEO, and COO. Mills argues, therefore, that
there is no distinct break with the old regime of entrepreneurial elites and thus Burnham's 'managerial revolution'
is a mirage. Burnham would argue that, in the case of William Clay Ford Jr., he trained as a managerial elite having
attended Princeton and MIT, and is thus a professional
manager whose roles have been *literally* interchangeable
with executives from Boeing and elsewhere who do not
carry the Ford name. Francis, however, argues:

> [I]t is largely irrelevant whether the propertied elite
> acquires managerial skills, takes an active part in
> managing corporate enterprise, or has assimilated
> non-propertied elite managers into its own class and
> interests. What Mills and [his disciple, William G.]
> Domhoff and their school do not sufficiently perceive
> or appreciate thoroughly is that the interests of the
> propertied elite have changed substantially with the
> revolution of mass and scale. The propertied elite or
> '*grand bourgeoise*' of the bourgeois order may not have
> changed significantly in family composition, and cer-
> tainly it retains wealth and status. Its economic in-
> terests, however, have changed from being vested in
> the hard property of privately owned and operated
> entrepreneurial firms, usually comparatively small
> in scale, to being intertwined with and dependent
> upon the dematerialized property of publicly owned,
> state-integrated, managerially operated mass corpo-

rations.[6]

In other words, whether or not a man of the propertied elite such as William Clay Ford Jr. takes an active or a passive role, his *interests* are now synonymous with the managerial regime while those of his great-grandfather were in many respects antagonistic to it. Francis argues that a family such as the Fords are now entirely dependent on managerial capitalism for their continued existence as propertied elites and are thus, in the final analysis, subordinated to the system. 'The propertied elite, the *grande bourgeoisie*, thus does not retain an economic interest in acting as the leader of the bourgeois order and defending its ideologies, values and institutions; its material interests push it toward defending the complex of managerial interests.'[7]

This perfectly explains why virtually none of the so-called *grand bourgeoisie* have taken a firm stance against what is today called 'woke capitalism'.[8] Whether they are propertied elites or not, executives who dare take a stance against the official managerial ideology are quickly removed, as was the case with Tripwire Interactive CEO and co-founder, John Gibson, who was forced to step down just 53 hours after tweeting his support for a ban on abortion in Texas.[9] Similarly, John Schattner, the founder of the Papa John's pizza chain—and a billionaire—was forced out of his own company by the board after making racially insensitive comments on a conference call in 2018.[10]

6   Francis, *Leviathan and Its Enemies*, p. 124.
7   Francis, *Leviathan and Its Enemies*, pp. 127–8.
8   Carl Rhodes, *Woke Capitalism: How Corporate Morality is Sabotaging Democracy* (Bristol: Bristol University Press, 2022).
9   Matt Egan, 'Video Game CEO is Out After Praising Texas Abortion Law', CNN (8 September 2021): https://edition.cnn.com/2021/09/07/business/tripwire-ceo-texas-abortion-law/index.html.
10   Ewan Palmer, 'Papa John's Founder John Schnatter Says Board Conspired to Oust Him, Vows "Day of Reckoning Will Come"',

Brendan Eich was forced to resign after only eleven days as CEO of Mozilla after it was found he had donated to a political campaign against gay marriage and employees launched a social media campaign to oust him.[11] I might continue listing examples such as these almost indefinitely, but there can be no doubt that Burnham and Francis are correct while Mills and Domhoff are wrong about whether power finally rests in the hands of the managers or the owner. The managers have primacy. If an owner does not adhere to managerial ideology—if the company in any way depends on managerial capitalism—they will find themselves removed in short order.

The second objection to Burnham with which Francis deals, is the idea that the managerial elite are not unified but rather a plurality. In fact, such objections were also applied to the work of Mills and his followers. Francis had in mind the work of Robert Dahl, David Truman, John Kenneth Galbraith, David Riesman, and Arnold M. Rose. As we have seen, Francis largely deals with this by acknowledging that while entry into the elite is possible its narrow and exclusively *managerial* character, which emphasises special qualifications and skills, in practice gives it a uniformity that is rare in history—he points out, citing Mosca, that the old capitalist entrepreneurial regime and even the old feudal system were much more diverse in terms of the makeup of the ruling class.[12] The third objection came from libertarians of the Reagan era who argued that the managerial regime is being eclipsed by the rise of newly-minted entrepreneurs. Today, minds may instinctively turn to a man like Bill Gates, or perhaps the Silicon

Newsweek (26 November, 2019): https://www.newsweek.com/papa-johns-john-schnatter-interview-1474073.

11   Alistair Barr, 'Mozilla CEO Brendan Eich Steps Down', The Wall Street Journal (3 April 2014): https://www.wsj.com/articles/mozilla-ceo-brendan-eich-to-step-down-1396554132.

12   Francis, *Leviathan and Its Enemies*, pp. 134–62, 660–5.

Valley types such as Mark Zuckerberg, Jack Dorsey, Elon Musk, and Peter Thiel. But virtually none of these billionaires are entrepreneurs in a manner that, say, Henry Ford was. They each made their fortunes by playing the system of the managerial regime and exploiting the 'fusion' of the state and the economy in one way or another. But even if there should spring forth a genuinely innovative and entrepreneurial firm, sooner or later, it becomes co-opted and is transformed into being part of the regime apparatus. Francis cites the example of McDonald's;[13] a more recent example might be Google.

Francis's major contribution to the general corpus of elite theory is in his emphasis on the role of ideology. Where Burnham emphasised the fusion of the state and corporations, as he put it 'managers-in-government' and 'managers-in-industry', Francis immediately recognised the importance of a third category of managers involved in opinion formation, which he called 'mass public relations' or 'mass organizations of culture and communication'. These include:

> [N]ot only the media of mass communication, one of the most important instruments by which the managerial elite disciplines and controls the mass population, but also all other mass organizations that disseminate, restrict, or invent information, ideas, and values advertising, publishing, journalism, film and broadcasting, entertainment, religion, education, and institutions for research and development. Indeed, the mass organizations of culture and communication, which generally lack the coercive disciplines of the mass corporation and the mass state, are able to provide disciplines and control for the mass population primarily through their use of the devices and techniques of mass communication. All the mass cultural organizations, then, function as part of the

13   Francis, *Leviathan and Its Enemies*, pp. 166–7.

media of mass communication, and they constitute a necessary element in the power base of the managerial elite.[14]

Francis was keenly aware of the ideological component of the managerial regime and his insights owe much to his deep understanding of the 'cultural turn' in Marxist literature after Antonio Gramsci, whom he cites.[15]

However—like both Burnham and Pareto—Francis saw ideology as mere justification for power, usually coming after the fact as a means of consolidation and control. This is to say that he saw the use of ideology as almost entirely cynical. In his 'Afterword' to *Leviathan and Its Enemies*, Paul Gottfried shares this revealing passage about his own fundamental disagreement with Francis:

> Sam and I would argue about his skepticism concerning whether elites accept their hegemonic ideas (in other words, whether elites really believe their own ideology). In his understanding of circulating elites, values and ideals were mere *instruments* for achieving practical goals; they advanced the interests of those seeking positions of authority. Sam would quote with pleasure the Italian economist and sociologist Vilfredo Pareto (1848–1923) that those involved in the power game would exploit whatever ideas and visions were most attractive to the masses in a particular culture. But, according to Sam, these elites would approach the myths as nothing more than ladders for their own ascent.[16]

This is, in fact, the old disagreement between Mosca and Pareto, about whether ideas affect history, restated. Gottfried occupies the Mosca position, while Francis takes the Pareto position. However, all four thinkers would ultimately agree

14   Francis, *Leviathan and Its Enemies*, pp. 11, 17.
15   Francis, *Leviathan and Its Enemies*, p. 75.
16   Paul E. Gottfried, 'Afterword', in *Leviathan and Its Enemies*, p. 738.

that the ideological *function* cannot be ignored in any analysis of power. The culture, even down to the everyday beliefs of the masses, must at some level reflect and 'buy into' the political formula of the ruling class.

Francis, however, recognised perhaps more than any other thinker that under the managerial regime the ideological vision must be totalising, which is to say no vestige of the previous regime can be allowed. He illustrates the point in a much livelier way than in *Leviathan and Its Enemies* in two pieces that were republished in the collection *Beautiful Losers*: 'The Cult of Dr King' and 'Equality as a Political Weapon'. In the former, he spots—in what has now become almost a commonplace insight—that the ideology of the managerial regime takes on an almost religious air with its own sacred heroes and symbols as embodied in the figure of Martin Luther King. While the symbolic significance of Christmas is fair game to debate politically every year, no such freedom is afforded to the annual celebration of Martin Luther King Day, which must be observed with solemn reverence and can only ever be about one thing: the righteous struggle of the Civil Rights movement. In a blistering conclusion, he writes:

> [Martin Luther King's] legacy, as its keepers know, is profoundly at odds with the historic American order, and that is why they can have no rest until the symbols of that order are pulled up root and branch. To say that Dr King and the cause he really represented are now part of the official American creed, indeed the defining and dominant symbol of that creed—which is what both houses of the United States Congress said in 1983 and what President Ronald Reagan signed into law shortly afterward—is the inauguration of a new order of the ages in which the symbols of the old order and the things they symbolized can retain neither meaning nor respect, in which they are as mute and dark as the gods of Babylon and Tyre,

and from whose cold ashes will rise a new god, level-
ling their rough places, straightening their crooked-
ness, and exalting every valley until the whole earth
is flattened beneath his feet and perceives the glory of
the new lord.[17]

What may have seemed like hyperbole in 1988 is an observed daily reality in the 2020s, when statues of everyone
from Confederates to Founding Fathers are physically torn
down by state-backed feral mobs with the full approval of every major corporation, university, and media outlet. In 2020,
after the Black Lives Matter protests following the death
of George Floyd, massive statues of Floyd were erected in
many public places across the USA, while Edinburgh University renamed 'David Hume Tower' to '40 George Square'
citing eighteenth-century Enlightenment philosopher's 'racist views'.[18] For Francis, such displays do not signal anything
more than the victory lap of the new order over the old order
which must be emptied of all significance.

In 'Equality as a Political Weapon', we see Francis's essential cynicism as regards actual belief in the doctrine of
equality. He seizes on a passage in Pareto:

> The sentiment that is very inappropriately named
> equality is fresh, strong, alert, precisely because it is
> not, in fact, a sentiment of equality and is not related
> to any abstraction, as a few naïve 'intellectuals' still
> believe; but because it is related to the direct inter-
> ests of individuals who are bent on escaping certain
> inequalities not in their favour, and setting up new
> inequalities that will be in their favour, this latter be-

---

17   Samuel T. Francis, 'The Cult of Dr King', in *Beautiful Losers:
Essays on the Failure of American Conservatism* (Columbia, MI: University of Missouri Press, 1993), p. 160.
18   'Edinburgh University renames David Hume Tower over
'racist' views', BBC News (13 September 2020): https://www.bbc.
co.uk/news/uk-scotland-edinburgh-east-fife-54138247.

ing their chief concern.[19]

One may think of any number of affirmative action programmes as an example of this, but it also brings to mind
the central logic of the Jouvenelian alliance between the
high and the low. The high can always promise to liberate
the low from 'oppressors' by promising to transfer advantages to them. Francis sees that this is little more than a
cynical power ploy:

> In the twentieth century, egalitarianism has been
> used principally as the political formula or ideolog-
> ical rationalization by which one, emerging elite has
> sought to displace from political, economic, and cul-
> ture power another elite, and in not only rational-
> izing but also disguising the dominance of the new
> elite.[20]

Francis points to the behaviourism of B. F. Skinner and
others, the belief in human beings as equal 'blank slates'
differentiated only by their upbringing, as one of the chief
strains of egalitarianism in the twentieth century:

> Egalitarianism played a central role in the progres-
> sivist ideological challenge, and the main form it
> assumed in the early twentieth century was that of
> 'environmentalism'—not in the contemporary sense
> of concern for ecology but in the sense that human
> beings are perceived as the products of their social
> and historical environment rather than of their in-
> nate mental and physical natures. [...] Indeed, the
> ideological function of progressivism in delegitimiz-
> ing bourgeois society was accomplished by its identi-

19   Vilfredo Pareto, *The Mind and Society*, ed. Arthur Livingstone,
trans. Andrew Bongiorno and Arthur Livingstone, 4 vols (1916;
New York: Harcourt, Brace and Company, 1935), vol 2, §1227, pp.
735–6.
20   Samuel T. Francis, 'Equality as a Political Weapon', in *Beautiful Losers*, p. 211.

fication of the society itself as the 'environment' to be altered through social management.[21]

The logic of environmentalism or behaviouralism thus always points in the direction of ever-increasing managerial control, since it is 'society' that must be changed, and such change can only take place through management.

Francis locates Edward Bernays as one of the chief culprits for inculcating this view among the elites in the 1920s and 1930s:

> Edward Bernays, a nephew of Sigmund Freud, also helped develop behaviourist psychological techniques for the managed economy in the science of 'public relations', which he helped found. 'Treating all people as mechanically identical', writes historian Stuart Ewen, Bernays, 'called for the implementation of a "mass psychology" by which public opinion might be controlled.'[22]

What is striking if one turns to Bernays is his naked and unapologetic elitism. In *Public Relations*, he speaks openly about 'The Engineering of Consent',[23] and warns leaders against following public attitude polls explicitly because they might hinder the progressive agenda:

> Society suffers when polls inhibit leaders from independent thinking, from anticipating change, or from preparing the public for change. [...] Polls exert pressure that may play society under what Jefferson called the tyranny of the majority and throttle progressive

21   Francis, 'Equality as a Political Weapon', pp. 213, 217.
22   Francis, 'Equality as a Political Weapon', p. 218. Quotation from Stuart Ewen, *Captains of Consciousness: Advertising and the Social Roots of the Consumer Culture* (New York: McGraw-Hill Book Company, 1976), p. 83.
23   Edward Bernays, 'The Engineering of Consent', in *Public Relations* (Norman, OK: University of Oklahoma Press, 1952), pp. 157–68.

minority ideas.[24]

Bernays does not see public opinion as something to be followed but something to be *managed* and, if necessary, transformed—preferably by using his services and expertise.

Bernays's fellow elitist, Walter Lippmann, was sceptical about the extent to which 'public opinion' even exists other than as a fabrication of the media—as a 'pseudo-environment'[25]—and wrote a book on this topic called *The Phantom Public*. It begins with a portrait of 'The Disenchanted Man', which is a neat summation of the passive masses:

> The private citizen today has come to feel rather like a deaf spectator in the back row, who ought to keep his mind on the mystery off there, but cannot quite manage to keep awake. He knows he is somehow affected by what is going on. Rules and regulations continually, taxes annually and wars occasionally remind him that he is being swept along by great drifts of circumstance. Yet these public affairs are in no convincing way his affairs. They are for the most part invisible. They are managed, if they are managed at all, at distant centers, from behind the scenes, by unnamed powers. As a private person he does not know for certain what is going on, or who is doing it, or where he is being carried. [...] In the cold light of experience he knows that his sovereignty is a fiction. He reigns in theory, but in fact does not govern.[26]

But Lippman does not, as one might imagine, lament this fact, but rather uses it as a call for a reign of experts—one might say, a managerial elite. He says:

24   Edward Bernays, 'Attitude Polls – Servants or Masters?' in *Public Relations*, p. 263.
25   Walter Lippmann, *Public Opinion* (New York: Harcourt, Brace & Co.: 1922), p. 17.
26   Walter Lippmann, *The Phantom Public* (1927; New York: Routledge, 2017), pp. 3–4.

I think it is a false ideal. I do not mean an undesirable
ideal. I mean an unattainable ideal, bad only in the
sense that it is bad for a fat man to try to be a ballet
dancer. An ideal should express the true possibilities
of its subject. When it does not it perverts the true
possibilities. The idea of the omnicompetent, sovereign citizen is, in my opinion, such a false ideal. It
is unattainable. The pursuit of it is misleading. The
failure to achieve it has produced the current disen-
chantment.[27]

Lippmann's solution is simply to do away with democratic
fictions and let the elites get on with the task of managing
their affairs:

[The thesis of *The Phantom Public*] does not assume
that men in action have universal purposes; they are
denied the fraudulent support of the fiction that they
are agents of a common purpose. They are regarded
as the agents of special purposes, without pretense
and without embarrassment. They must live in a
world with men who have other special purposes.
[...] I have no legislative program to offer, no new
institutions to propose. There are, I believe, immense
confusions in the current theory of democracy which
frustrate and pervert its action.[28]

The role of the public is simply to rubber stamp which
party of the elites gets to govern, even if there is little difference between the choices on offer:

Although it is the custom of partisans to speak as if
there were radical differences between the Ins and
Outs, it could be demonstrated, I believe, that in stable and mature societies the differences are not profound. If they were profound, the defeated minority
would be constantly on the verge of rebellion. An

27   Lippmann, *The Phantom Public*, p. 29.
28   Lippmann, *The Phantom Public*, pp. 188, 190.

election would be catastrophic, whereas the assumption in every election is that the victors will do nothing to make life intolerable to the vanquished and that the vanquished will endure with good humour policies which they do not approve.[29]

In the 2020s, it is perfectly clear that, according to Lippmann's criteria, the USA is no longer a 'stable and mature' society. Lippmann viewed the masses as a 'bewildered herd' whose opinions needed to be 'managed only by a specialized class whose personal interests reach beyond the locality',[30] in other words by men like Edward Bernays. However, it strikes me that this narrow vision of democracy as a mere rubber stamp of rule by experts who engage in 'perception management' is running towards its death throes. This is primarily because the internet—a modern Gutenberg Press—has destroyed the ability of elites to control narratives, which is causing them to become more desperate, coercive, and brittle. As more people come to see them as unmistakably totalitarian in nature, and as the gap between elite and popular values widens, it is only a matter of time until we see a circulation of elites because the managerial regime is failing precisely at the moment of its apparent victory lap.

A near perfect illustration of this failure of narrative control took place in early January 2022. On December 31 2021, Joe Rogan interviewed Dr Robert Malone—the inventor of the nine original mRNA vaccine patents, the author of nearly 100 peer-reviewed papers with over 12,000 citations—for three hours, during which he highlighted many unanswered questions about the COVID-19 vaccine.[31] In addition to the interview, Dr Malone leads a coalition of over 16,000 doctors and scientists 'dedicated to

29   Lippmann, *The Phantom Public*, p. 117.
30   Lippmann, *Public Opinion*, p. 204.
31   The Joe Rogan Experience, '#1757 – Dr Robert Malone, MD' (31 December 2021): https://open.spotify.com/episode/3SCsueX-2bZdbEzRtKOCEyT.

speaking truth to power'.[32] Madhava Setty, MD, who also holds a degree in electrical engineering from MIT, then asked whether this was the 'most important interview of our time'.[33] The interview was promptly banned by You-Tube and Twitter, who suspended any attempts to upload it, and Dr Malone was personally banned from Twitter.[34] Defenders of the regime such as Dr Dan Wilson—whose video was pushed to the front of the algorithm by Google's managers in perception—quickly denounced Dr Malone as having gone 'full anti-science'.[35] Legacy mainstream media outlets quickly set to work to 'debunk' Dr Malone, who—despite his obvious credentials—was said to have 'no academic credibility' by 'experts' and reported breathlessly by twenty-something journalists in well-known and once respected newspapers.[36] Then CNN ran a piece hosted by Brian Stelter entitled 'Is the Media Out of Touch with the Country over COVID?' Stelter's colleague, Oliver Darcy, said:

32   He is President of the Global Covid Summit: https://global-covidsummit.org/.

33   Madhava Setty, 'Rogan and Malone: Most Important Interview of Our Time?', The Defender (4 January 2022): https://childrenshealthdefense.org/defender/joe-rogan-robert-malone-interview-covid-vaccine/.

34   Shannon Thaler, 'YouTube and Twitter Delete Joe Rogan Interview with Scientist who Helped Invent mRNA Vaccines', Daily Mail (3 January, 2022): https://www.dailymail.co.uk/news/article-10364679/YouTube-Twitter-delete-Joe-Rogan-interview-scientist-helped-invent-MRNA-vaccines.html.

35   Debunk the Flunk with Dr Wilson, 'Robert Malone Goes Full Anti-Science on Joe Rogan's Podcast', YouTube (5 January 2022): https://www.youtube.com/watch?v=xjszVOfG_wo.

36   Gino Spocchia, ''No Academic Credibility': Experts Debunk Mass Psychosis Covid theory Floated by Doctor on Joe Rogan Podcast', The Independent (10 January 2022): https://www.independent.co.uk/news/world/americas/covid-psychosis-theory-joe-rogan-b1989552.html.

> A lot of the media does seem, as I look at it, and travel the country, to be very out of touch with people. I mean if you travel the country, people are not really living in the same bubble [...] it seems that the media is messaging toward. [...] And so, I think this is an issue, because if people are tuning out what's going on in Cable News, if we're not messaging towards the general population, then they're just ignoring everything and living their lives [...] and we're not really getting the information that they need to them.[37]

From the standpoint of what we have been discussing as regards managerial elites, this episode is remarkable for at least three reasons. First, it is obvious that Dr Malone and his band of 16,000 doctors and scientists are managerial elites by the classic Burnham definition—*technical experts*—and they have broken decisively with the regime over its management of the pandemic. Second, Joe Rogan's podcast has become more watched and listened to than CNN or any other legacy media outlet—to the extent that one might question whether the labels 'alternative' and 'mainstream' are still appropriate. Third, the managerial masters of persuasion openly complained that their 'messaging' is not working and that, in effect, no one is listening to them. If only the White House or CNN could hire Edward Bernays maybe things might be different—but one suspects that even if Bernays himself was managing this, he could do nothing about the loss of monopoly control over information flow that has been caused by the internet.

Let us return to Francis who longed for a 'revolution from the middle' and saw its scope in what he called 'the post-bourgeois resistance' made up of the middle classes—including 'kulaks' or *petite bourgeois*—the lower middle

---

37   Video excerpt can be found on Zack Heilman, 'CNN Accidentally Admits Their 'News' Isn't Working, People Are Just Living Their Lives, Ignoring Us', Red Voice Media (10 January 2022): https://www.redvoicemedia.com/2022/01/cnn-accidentally-admits-their-news-isnt-working-people-are-just-living-their-lives-ignoring-us/.

class and the working class. This is a straightforward 'foxes versus lions', or Class I residues vs. Class II residues, analysis derived from Pareto's strong influence on Francis's thinking:

> Post-bourgeois groups manifest hostility not only to the ideology of the soft managerial regime and to the psychic and behavioural patterns of its elite but also to the manipulative style of dominance that characterizes the elite and the tendency to acceleration on which the elite relies for the preservation and enhancement of its power. The managerial use of manipulation and acceleration not only alienates post-bourgeois groups culturally and morally but also threatens their economic position and social status.[38]

When commentators say that Francis 'predicted' the rise of Donald Trump, it was for passages like this, in which he perfectly encapsulates the essential problem. It does not appear that Francis was aware of Jouvenel's work, but he spots the alliance between elites and 'the underclass, particularly its non-white components'.[39] Although Francis could not have foreseen the rise of the internet, he recognises several vulnerabilities in the managerial regime. Drawing from Mosca, he views the fact that the elite are monolithic and uniform as being a weakness, which is ironic given their famous slogan 'diversity is our strength':

> The formal mechanisms of mass liberal democracy—regular elections, competing political parties, universal suffrage, and legal and political rights—do not significantly mitigate the monolithic and uniform concentration of managerial power. [...] The 'despotism' of the regime—its tendency toward the monopolization of political, economic, and cultural power by a single social and political force of managerial and

38 Francis, *Leviathan and Its Enemies*, p. 576.
39 Francis, *Leviathan and Its Enemies*, p. 588.

technical skills and the expansive, uniform, and centralized nature of its power—is a direct consequence of the contracted composition of the elite and the restriction of its membership to elements proficient in managerial and technical skills [...] The narrowness of the elite that results from this restriction insulates it from the influence of non-managerial social and political forces and reduces their ability to gain positions within the elite from which they can moderate, balance, or restrain its commands [...] their exclusion from the elite contributes to the frustration of their aspirations and interests and encourages their alienation from and conflict with the elite and the destabilization and weakening of the regime.[40]

This destabilization takes the form of decomposition and fragmentation in the social order, which we have undoubtedly witnessed in the three decades since Francis was writing. Since the managerial regime is 'soft' and frequently does not actually solve problems but opts rather simply to 'manage perception' or 'engineer consent', it seems likely that de facto balkanisation will begin to occur in both the USA and Europe. So-called 'No-Go Zones', in which the authorities have essentially given up policing have already emerged in major cities.[41] While these have, to date, occurred in non-white areas populated by 'the underclass', as post-bourgeois white populations become more disaffected by managerial elite rule, and even if they come to distrust the authorities themselves, it is perfectly possible that de facto autonomous 'No-Go Zones' could occur in white areas too. In the USA, both the Trump and Biden presidencies have been characterised by widespread state-level non-compliance with federal and executive edicts. If half the country declare that the President is 'not my president' no matter who wins the election, the regime has a serious problem on its hands. As I have mentioned

40   Francis, *Leviathan and Its Enemies*, p. 662, 667–8.
41   Raheem Kassam, *No Go Zones: How Sharia Law Is Coming to a Neighborhood Near You* (Washington, DC: Regnery, 2017).

previously, the current strategy of simply writing off thirty percent or more of the population as 'undesirables' simply cannot serve. In Mosca's terms, there is a lack of 'moral unity' between the rulers and the ruled, and historically this situation has not and will not persist for long.[42]

42   Gaetano Mosca, *The Ruling Class*, ed. Arthur Livingston, trans. Hannah D. Khan (1895; New York: McGraw-Hill, 1939), p. 10.

Chapter 9
THE THERAPEUTIC STATE

In theory, the role of government is not for the sake of its own power, but for the benefit of the people it is supposed to serve. If a government does not serve the people, then it must be transformed until it does so or be overthrown and replaced with one which does. However, in *Multiculturalism and the Politics of Guilt*, published in 2002, Paul Gottfried argued that the modern managerial regime had completely inverted this theoretical relationship. Rather than transforming itself to serve the people, the managerial regime seeks to *transform people* in the service of its system of atomised corporate consumerism. It drives ever more closely towards what Jouvenel saw as the final destination:

> It ends [...] in the disappearance of every constraint which does not emanate from the state, and in the denial of every pre-eminence which is not approved by the state. In a word, it ends in the atomization of society, and in the rupture of every private tie linking man and man, whose only bond is now their common bondage to the state. The extremes of individualism and socialism meet: that was their predestined course.[1]

1   Bertrand de Jouvenel, *On Power: The Natural History of Its Growth*, trans. J.F. Huntington (1945; Minneapolis, MN: Liberty

However, Gottfried identifies the root of this not in managerialism per se, which is simply the vehicle through which its ends are achieved, but in two proximate causes: multiculturalism, which is to say, the prevalence of minority groups whose 'political efforts go [...] towards neutralizing the cultural and institutional particularities associated with a majority out-group,' and a religious and cultural phenomenon owing chiefly to a progressive perversion of mainline Protestant churches that manifests itself as white guilt. This results in an atmosphere to which white people must submit in self-abasement and atonement for past sins. It necessitates, 'the grafting on to administrative states of therapeutic and punitive agencies for forming social consciousness and chastising those with defective sensibility.'[2]

By now political correctness and its causes are well-worn themes. It has also become a commonplace to identify modern 'social justice' and its dominant theme of 'white guilt' as a kind of religion. Gottfried arrived at such conclusions at least twenty years before most commentators, as did Sam Francis, whose work we have already explored. The specific causes are incidental to our purposes here, but it is worth listing them. Gottfried sees the issue as predominantly American, arising from the so-called melting pot, and then exported to the rest of the Anglosphere from the mid-1960s onwards who 'came to imitate the crusade against discrimination then being waged across the Atlantic'. In the American milieu, the key groups are the so-called WASPs (White Anglo-Saxon Protestants), who have allowed their mainline churches to stray very far from Biblical teachings to general sermonising about the dangers of bigotry, and an alliance of minority groups which include Jews, Irish and Italian Catholics, and blacks.

2   Paul E. Gottfried, *Multiculturalism and The Politics of Guilt: Toward a Secular Theocracy* (Columbia, MI: University of Missouri Press, 2002), pp. 42, 43.

Gottfried locates at heart of the issue: 'the feminization of Christianity [...] the fusion of a victim-centred feminism with the Protestant framework of sin and redemption.'[3] It is not difficult to see a perverted form of the Calvinist doctrine of Absolute Depravity in contemporary social justice rhetoric. I recall being at an international conference in 2017 at which a world-famous feminist Renaissance scholar at Columbia—undoubtedly a WASP—spoke for almost half an hour in unmistakably religious terms about her 'shame' at being white. In truth, I could not bear to witness this act of public penance and left the conference hall after ten minutes.

Gottfried does not solely lay blame on Protestantism gone awry. He also points to the political games played by minority groups. Gottfried, who is Jewish, notes the 'double standard', for example, of Jews 'who combine strong nationalist feelings for their own group and for Israel with the advocacy of open borders, alternative lifestyles, and extreme pluralism for their host countries.'[4] Elsewhere, around the time he was writing *Multiculturalism and the Politics of Guilt*, he noted the weaponization of social-justice rhetoric by Jewish groups against their chief political rivals, the white Christian Right:

> But seeking out bloc alliances with blacks and other 'marginalized' groups is thought to help American Jews in another, more significant way. Like gays and feminists, blacks are valuable for those who perceive the white Christian Right as their major enemy and as the prime source of American anti-Semitism. I would urge Professor Forman to look at the Anti-Defamation League's 1994 publication, *The Religious Right: The Assault on Tolerance and Pluralism in America*, as an illustration of how leading American Jewish organizations perceive their 'self-interest.'

3 Gottfried, *Multiculturalism and The Politics of Guilt*, pp. 45, 55–6.
4 Gottfried, *Multiculturalism and The Politics of Guilt*, p. 41.

It is by declaring solidarity with blacks and others thought to be on the Left, against the predominantly Southern-based Religious Right. 'Racist,' 'theocracy,' 'Holocaust denier,' and 'anti-abortion' are becoming interchangeable terms in American Jewish tirades against the Christian Right. Remaining firmly tied to blacks is therefore seen as necessary to preserve Jews against the real enemy, the one they fear and detest most whether or not it poses a real threat to their individual or communal existence.[5]

However, Gottfried notes that other minority groups have played these political games too, including Irish and Italian Catholics. Of course, good students of elite theory would not be surprised in the slightest that in a multicultural liberal democracy tightly organised special interest groups should come to dominate the disorganised majority: this is Mosca's Law.

What troubles Gottfried most is that the manufacturing of consent that we have already discussed has now been pathologised and even medicalised. He suggests that since the 1960s, the 'behaviour modification' and social engineering programs of the managerial state have relentlessly fought against 'discrimination' and promoted 'diversity' using the looming image of the Nazis or the ghosts of slavery and the segregationist South as cudgels in a permanent slippery slope argument. He identifies three tactics that are routinely employed. First, the tendency of media and other opinion-makers to stress that 'consensus has already been reached, for example, over immigration or multicultural programs'.[6] In the UK, the BBC would routinely engage in this form of gaslighting on its flagship debate show, *Question Time*. They would routinely present a panel with four pro-immigration voices against a lone anti-immigration

5   Paul E. Gottfried, 'The Black-Jewish Alliance', *Academic Questions*, 14:3 (Summer 2001), p. 7.
6   Gottfried, *Multiculturalism and the Politics of Guilt*, pp. 72–3.

voice. The studio crowd would cheer the pro-immigration voices and boo the anti-immigration voice. This serves to isolate the viewer at home watching the show who may be against immigration by creating *the perception* that their stance is held by a despised minority. In fact, from 1964 to 2017 over 65% of the British public opposed immigration according to the *British Election Study*.[7] The media nakedly employs a persuasion tool known as 'social proof' in a bid to make the public more accepting of mass immigration.[8] The second tactic Gottfried identifies is 'employing the past as a club': 'By harping on the real or imagined evils of the past, proponents of state-controlled socialization appeal to the guilty conscious of their listeners [...] and furnish occasions for exhibitions of public righteousness.'[9] Such exhibitions have become by now so routine and widespread that they have gained the label 'virtue signalling'.[10]

However, the third and most insidious method is to treat the unwanted behaviour as a form of sickness, 'to depict unfashionable thinkers and retrograde views as "pathological"'. Gottfried is rightly perturbed at the implications of treating 'dissent as a form of mental illness' which requires psychiatric remedy.[11] This pathologizing tendency has its

7   See Scott Blinder and Lindsay Richards, 'UK Public Opinion toward Immigration: Overall Attitudes and Level of Concern', The Migration Observatory (20 January 2020): https://migrationobservatory.ox.ac.uk/resources/briefings/uk-public-opinion-toward-immigration-overall-attitudes-and-level-of-concern/, figure 2.

8   On 'social proof' see Robert B. Cialdini, *Influence: The Psychology of Persuasion* (1984; New York: William Morrow, 2007), pp. 144–66.

9   Gottfried, *Multiculturalism and the Politics of Guilt*, p. 73.

10   The phrase was popularly coined in James Bartholomew, 'The Awful Rise of "Virtue Signalling"', The Spectator (April 18, 2015): https://www.spectator.co.uk/2015/04/hating-the-daily-mail-is-a-substitute-for-doing-good/.

11   Gottfried, *Multiculturalism and the Politics of Guilt*, p. 73.

overt post-war roots in the work of the Frankfurt School
and specifically Theodor W. Adrono's *The Authoritarian
Personality Type*.[12] Gottfried gives a full treatment to this
text in his earlier book *After Liberalism*, to which *Multiculturalism and the Politics of Guilt* was a sequel.[13] Elsewhere, he
is at pains to point out that contrary to certain right-wing
conspiracy theories which suggest that the injection of
Frankfurt School thinking into Western institutions was
a Marxist plot hatched from Moscow, that Adorno 'was
sponsored by an emphatically liberal but also anti-Sovi-
et sponsor, the American Jewish Committee.'[14] In other
words, this is not *subversion* of liberalism by communist
agitators, this is the *logic* of managerial liberalism played
out to its natural limits.

In *After Liberalism*, drawing on Thomas Szasz and Christopher Lasch,[15] he charts how the fields of psychiatry and
psychology gave rise to a new expert class whose role was
to regulate, alter, and normalise behaviour to conform to
the requirements of managerialism:

> The invasion of government and the courts by be-
> havioral scientists has produced what Thomas Szasz
> calls 'the therapeutic state.' Psychiatrists and social
> psychologists have been given social status, accord-

12   Theordor W. Adorno, *The Authoritarian Personality* (New
York: Harper & Brothers, 1950).
13   Paul E. Gottfried, *After Liberalism: Mass Democracy in the Managerial State* (Princeton, NJ: Princeton University Press, 1999), pp.
91–4.
14   Paul E. Gottfried, 'The Frankfurt School and Cultural Marxism', American Thinker (12 January 2018): https://www.ameri-
canthinker.com/articles/2018/01/the_frankfurt_school_and_cul-
tural_marxism.html.
15   See Thomas Szasz, *Law, Liberty and Psychiatry* (New York:
Macmillan, 1963); *The Myth of Mental Illness* (New York: Harper &
Row, 1961); and *Psychiatric Justice* (New York: Macmillan, 1965);
Christopher Lasch, *The True and Only Heaven: Progress and Its Critics*
(New York: W. W. Norton, 1991).

ing to Szasz, and their moral and political judgments, though not always founded on hard, empirical science, are taken to be 'expert.' These experts today can affect decisions about the responsibility of criminals, the right to control property, and the custody of children. 'Psychiatric theologians' have been able to impose their private political opinions as 'scientific' truth, and Szasz cites the fact that the American Psychiatric Association now defines the involuntary treatment and incarceration of mental patients as 'health rights.' Szasz also observes, 'If people believe that health values justify coercion, but that moral and political do not, those who wish to coerce others will tend to enlarge the category of health values at the expense of moral values.' 'Health values' have also become socialized through a global managerial culture. Since 1976 the United Nations, through its International Covenant on Economic, Cultural, and Social Rights, has elevated 'the enjoyment of the highest standard [...] of mental health' to a sacred entitlement. Henceforth governments must ensure a sound state of mind as a 'human right.'[16]

It is interesting that this analysis of the relationship between the field of mental health and power has a parallel on the left in the work of Michel Foucault.[17] Foucault pointed how the 'medical' or 'clinical' gaze obscures the functioning of power because of the morally neutral language of science. However, as much as Foucault is added to university reading lists and read by undergraduates, it seems that no one at universities, least of all those on the left, ever stops to question the relationship between power and public and mental health in the current paradigm. One might suggest that this is because they now see themselves in power. Instead of using Foucault to criticise the current

16   Paul E. Gottfried, *After Liberalism*, p. 79.
17   Michel Foucault, *Madness and Civilization*, trans. Richard Howard (1961; New York and London: Routledge, 2010).

paradigm, they seem to remain frozen forever analysing the culture of the 1950s and deconstructing the last one. Gottfried continues:

> Christopher Lasch explains the process by which the therapeutic segment of the managerial elite won moral acceptance. Despite the fact that its claims to be providing 'mental health' were always self-serving and highly subjective, the therapeutic class offered ethical leadership in the absence of shared principles. By defining emotional well-being as both a social good and the overcoming of what is individually and collectively dangerous, the behavioral scientists have been able to impose their absolutes upon a culturally fluid society. In *The True and Only Heaven* Lasch explores the implications for postwar politics of the *Authoritarian Personality*. A chief contributor to this anthology, Theodor Adorno, abandoned his earlier work as a cultural critic to become a proponent of governmentally imposed social therapy. According to Lasch, Adorno condemns undesirable political attitudes as 'prejudice,' and 'by defining prejudice as a "social disease" substituted a medical for a political idiom.' In the end, Adorno and his colleagues 'relegated a broad range of controversial issues to the clinic—to scientific study as opposed to philosophical and political debate.'[18]

As per Carl Schmitt, there are no neutral institutions including medical or psychiatric institutions. If the managerial state makes anti-discrimination the moral centre of its political formula, then discriminatory views are diagnosed as mentally abnormal. In such a regime, 'unconscious bias training' is mandated at most workplaces and for employees of the state despite empirical proof that it does not even achieve the behaviour modification at which it aims, by admission of the British Government. The UK Cabinet Office's 'Written

18   Paul E. Gottfried, *After Liberalism*, p. 80.

Statement on Unconscious Bias Training', ostensibly written in the neutral language of science, concludes by reaffirming its commitment to the political formula of the therapeutic state: Equality, Diversity and Inclusion: 'The Civil Service will therefore integrate principles for inclusion and diversity into mainstream core training and leadership modules in a manner which facilitates positive behaviour change.'[19] Here is an open declaration that the state is engaged in 'positive behaviour change' as a central mission. At the time of writing, the former UK Prime Minister, Tony Blair, speaking in an interview with CNN, said, 'it's an indicator of how broken politics has been that the issue of vaccination should become political. I mean, it's just a question of science.'[20] One might ask Mr Blair how the issue of having one's body penetrated by a foreign object by order of the government could ever *not* be political.

It is important for us to grasp here the salient feature of Gottfried's analysis, which is not merely to say that the managerial state has developed and adopted this ideology and these tools of mass manipulation to justify its own power, but also that it has developed them as a *political weapon*:

> [T]he political class has adopted inclusiveness and diversity as a political instrument, as a means of controlling a society it has set about reshaping. [...] the 'diversity machine' is a mechanism of state power that operates without anyone being permitted to notice its coercive nature. Therapeutic regimes are packaged in a way that disguises their resort to force;

19   UK Cabinet Office, 'Written Ministerial Statement on Unconscious Bias Training', Gov.uk (17 December 2020): https://www.gov.uk/government/news/written-ministerial-statement-on-unconscious-bias-training.
20   Christiane Amanpour, 'Blair: Britain's Political Relationship with America Isn't Strong Anymore', CNN (22 January 2022): https://edition.cnn.com/videos/tv/2022/01/21/amanpour-tony-blair-future-of-britain-ukraine.cnn.

> both the Left and establishment Right in the United
> States, which misrepresent political life, have helped
> to make this concealment possible.[21]

Thus, insidious efforts at social engineering are shrouded
in a cloak of benevolence. In managerial doublespeak, flat-
ly coercive programs are cast as vehicles for 'empowerment'.
One is reminded of when Bob Dylan sings, 'Good intentions
can be evil / Both hands can be full of grease / You know
that sometimes Satan comes as a man of peace.'[22] Every moral revolution expands the realm of managerial control: 'The
government now in place [...] searches out radical forces in
order to break down "noninclusive" behavioural patterns and
to subjugate citizens. Those who favour such a course, for
individual or collective reasons, will empower the state to
pursue it.' The most blatant example of this in recent years
has been the borderline insane push to recognise transgender
men and women as being indistinguishable from so-called
'cis' men and women. The public maintenance of obvious
fictions and falsehoods signals allegiance and obedience to
the regime and serves no other function whatsoever than
to punish dissidents. The most famous example of this has
been the attempted unpersoning of the otherwise pristinely
politically correct liberal J. K. Rowling for her alleged 'trans-
phobia'. Controversy surrounding her failure to abide by the
new managerial edict to recognise biological men who take
hormone supplements and wear skirts as women and biological women who take testosterone supplements and wear
masculine clothing as men has led to, among other things, a
school dropping her name from a building,[23] and her virtual

21   Gottfried, *Multiculturalism and the Politics of Guilt*, p. 79.
22   Bob Dylan, 'Man of Peace', on *Infidels* (New York: Columbia
Records, 1983).
23   See Dan Sales, 'JK Rowling is Cancelled Again: Performing
Arts School Drops Harry Potter Author's name from House over
Her Views on Transgender Rights', Daily Mail (4 January 2022):
https://www.dailymail.co.uk/news/article-10367133/JK-Rowl-
ing-cancelled-Performing-arts-school-drops-Harry-Potter-au-

erasure from a twenty-year *Harry Potter* reunion.[24]

In 2002, Gottfried predicted, correctly as it turned out, that the ever-widening chasm between the 'equality, diversity and inclusion' doctrine of the therapeutic state and the lived reality and beliefs of most ordinary people would result in a populist backlash against managerial overreach. He claimed that the regime faces a 'paradigm crisis' in which 'the gap between its democratic and liberal self-descriptions and its imposed social policies' would become too obvious to escape notice and therefore 'the efforts to justify these policies with archaic terminology or human rights rhetoric no longer elicit widespread belief.'[25] At the time of writing, a recent study by the University of Chicago has found that 47 million Americans are said to believe that the 2020 Election was stolen; 21 million believe that Joe Biden is not a legitimate president, '63% of people agree with the statement that "African American people or Hispanic people in our country will eventually have more rights than whites"—a belief sometimes called "the Great Replacement"', and '54% agree that "A secret group of Satan-worshipping pedophiles is ruling the US government," which is the key belief in the QAnon movement.'[26] A more recent poll has found that one in three Americans believe that violence against the government is justified.[27]

thor-transgender-row.html.

24   George Simpson, 'JK Rowling's "Prominent Absence' from Harry Potter Reunion "like not inviting The Queen"', Daily Express (29 December 2021): https://www.express.co.uk/entertainment/films/1542583/JK-Rowling-absence-Harry-Potter-reunion-Return-to-Hogwarts-reviews.

25   Gottfried, *Multiculturalism and the Politics of Guilt*, p. 135.

26   Robert A. Pape, '21 Million Americans say Biden is "Illegitimate" and Trump should be Restored by Violence, Survey Finds', Opinion Today (21 September 2021): https://opiniontoday.com/2021/09/23/21-million-americans-say-biden-is-illegitimate-and-trump-should-be-restored-by-violence-survey-finds/.

27   Martin Pengelly, 'One in Three Americans Say Violence

Mosca's warning that no ruling class can remain a ruling class for long if the masses do not buy into its political formula seems to ring ever louder.

Where Francis took his cues chiefly from Burnham and Pareto, Gottfried's chief influence was Carl Schmitt and in particular the 'primacy of the political'. The idea that we could ever reach 'the end of history' has been shown to be nonsense. But Gottfried stresses that a peculiar feature of therapeutic managerialism is its need to maintain the fiction of consensus—previous ruling classes had no such requirement and had more actual diversity of opinion within their ranks. However, to function properly, the therapeutic state requires 'the downplaying of genuine political differences.'[28] The sorts of characters who attend the Davos Agenda hosted by the World Economic Forum—the most elite managers of today—speak in the language of consensus. One such character, Larry Fink, the CEO of Blackrock, who manages over $7.5 trillion in assets and who can name the US Federal Reserve as a client, uses phrases such as 'public-private partnership' and stresses that it is important for CEOs across all businesses to be unified, it has 'never been more essential for CEOs to have a consistent voice'.[29] Although he speaks in gushing terms about the 'power of capitalism', it is quickly clear that Fink's message is managerial and that his vision is for a quasi-command economy in which the controllers of capital dictate the investment agenda for the future:

> Every company and every industry will be trans-

Against the Government is Justified – Poll', The Guardian (2 January 2022): https://www.theguardian.com/us-news/2022/jan/02/one-three-americans-violence-government-justified-poll.

28   Gottfried, *Multiculturalism and the Politics of Guilt*, p. 140.
29   Larry Fink, 'Larry Fink's 2022 Letter to CEOs: The Power of Capitalism', Blackrock (January 2022): https://www.blackrock.com/corporate/investor-relations/larry-fink-ceo-letter.

formed by the transition to a net zero world. The
question is, will you lead, or will you be led? [...] We
focus on sustainability not because we're environ-
mentalists, but because we are capitalists and fidu-
ciaries to our clients. [...] Divesting from entire sectors—or simply passing carbon-intensive assets from
public markets to private markets—will not get the
world to net zero. [...] When we harness the power
of both the public and private sectors, we can achieve
truly incredible things. This is what we must do to
get to net zero.[30]

Simply put, this is *not capitalism*, this is agenda setting
whereby one of the most powerful executives in the world
announces five-year and ten-year plans for 'what the future will look like' in an almost entirely top-down managed economy. This language of *consensus* conceals the truly *political* character of what Fink is saying. In fact, he has
the temerity to start his letter by saying that:

COVID-19 has also deepened the erosion of trust in
traditional institutions and exacerbated polarization
in many Western societies. This polarization pres-
ents a host of new challenges for CEOs. Political ac-
tivists, or the media, may politicize things your company does. They may hijack your brand to advance
their own agendas. In this environment, facts themselves are frequently in dispute, but businesses have
an opportunity to lead.[31]

Thus when he sets his 'net zero carbon' agenda later, it is cast
in the politically neutral language of inevitability. But in actuality, his letter contains an explicit threat: if CEOs do not get
on board with this agenda they will be 'left behind', they will
be identified as the enemies of progress and someone—perhaps someone whose company owns half the exchange-trad-
ed funds in the world—might see to it that these enemies no

30   Fink, '2022 Letter to CEOs'.
31   Fink, '2022 Letter to CEOs'.

longer have a seat at the table. In theory 'the market' decides, but in practice, men like Larry Fink decide. A company can now be sunk regardless of its actual success with consumers simply through investor activism. Likewise, products that have little to no market demand such as Beyond Meat can be thrust onto the shelves despite continually failing to sell;[32] appalling sales figures have not stopped massive corporations such as McDonalds and KFC pushing Beyond Meat 'plant burgers' to the front and centre of their menus using the full might of their advertising budgets.

Most of this attempted engineering of consent by the therapeutic regime serves the purpose of identifying Schmittian friends and enemies. The list of enemy terms which serve to expel you from employment and society at large continues to expand: sexist, racist, homophobe, transphobe, climate denier, 'unvaccinated', and so on. These are all markers of ideological impurity which serve to dehumanise: 'ideologically conscripted armies tended more and more to demonize their targets. Those who re-sisted the ideal embodied by one's nation were no longer viewed as human in thinking or in fact.'[33] In the Twentieth Century, this resulted in catastrophic total wars between managerial states. After the collapse of the Soviet Union, the USA, under the neo-conservatives, continued a cru-sade to spread liberal democracy to all parts of the world and to dissolve any vestiges of outmoded traditions with a missionary zeal. As these efforts were frustrated, and as populations ever-more started to turn against such war-mongering, the missionary zeal turned *inwards*. Where in the 1990s and 2000s, so many ersatz Hitlers resided in Ser-bia, Iraq, Iran, North Korea and so on, in the 2020s, they

32   Hilary Russ and Nivedita Balu, 'Beyond Meat Loss Exceeds Forecasts on Higher Costs, Slow Restaurant Sales', Reuters (6 May 2021), ' https://www.reuters.com/business/retail-consumer/be-yond-meat-quarterly-revenue-misses-estimates-2021-05-06/.
33   Gottfried, *Multiculturalism and the Politics of Guilt*, p. 138.

are at home: not simply the despised Donald Trump, but also his supporters, and now people who refuse to submit to the prescribed remedies of the COVID-19 pandemic. In time it will no doubt encompass meat eaters, people who wish to drive petrol-fuelled cars, and so on. The question remains whether societies can function while around 30% of the productive population are demonised and dehumanized in this way. This has never been achieved in history by any ruling class. Stalin and other such dictators simply opted to eliminate their enemies through brute force: they were willing to do so to consolidate power and control. Managerial elites seem unwilling to use such force and instead must rely on increasingly transparent games of perception management. At least by the estimation of Ngaire Woods, speaking at the World Economic Forum in November 2021, our current ruling elites seem to be aware of their own unpopularity. At an event called 'The Great Narrative, she said:

> At Davos a few years ago, the Edelman survey showed us that the good news is the elite across the world trust each other more and more, so we can come together and design and do beautiful things together. The bad news is that in every single country they were polling, the majority of people trusted that elite less.[34]

The World Economic Forum's *Global Risks Report* for 2022 lists 'social cohesion' as a major concern and notes that 'A recent poll in the United States, for example, found "division in the country" to be voters' top concern: they expected it to worsen in 2022.'[35] While Gottfried in 2002 was unwilling to

---

34   Ngaire Woods, 'The Great Narrative: A Call to Action', World Economic Forum, Dubai (12 November 2021): https://www.weforum.org/events/the-great-narrative-2021/sessions/closing-plenary-03768dee1f.
35   World Economic Forum, The Global Risks Report 2022 (Da-

predict their ultimate demise, it seems to me that unless the current ruling class is prepared to become openly coercive and use force, it will be overthrown once counter-elites become organised enough to do so in every region and locality.

vos: World Economic Forum, 2022), p. 17.

Chapter 10
CONCLUSION

The thesis of this book has been that democracy is and always has been an illusion, in which the true functioning of power where an organised minority elite rule over a disorganised mass is obscured through a lie that 'the people is sovereign'. I have called this 'the populist delusion' because of the number of other lies that this central lie conceals, chiefly the myth of bottom-up power or 'people power' and the entirely inaccurate view of history this lie creates. There is never a substitute for the tightly organised minority. This fact, Mosca's law, is the key lesson of the Italian elite theorists: Gaetano Mosca, Vilfredo Pareto and Robert Michels. I believe that the outbreak of populism in Europe and America that started in 2015 was significantly stymied due to a view of power and the functioning of Western systems that was wholly wrong, which is to say that the people who made up those populist movements believed re-articulations of a false political formula that they were taught in their civics or history classes at school. The myth of social change being a 'bottom-up' phenomenon pervades our culture and thinking. It is the essential fiction of 1960s counterculture and the worldview of the baby boomers.

It is worth returning to the four myths of liberalism that help to perpetuate this worldview:

1. *Myth of the stateless society:* that state and society

were or could ever be separate.

2. *Myth of the neutral state:* that state and politics were or could ever be separate.

3. *Myth of the free market:* that state and economy were or could ever be separate.

4. *Myth of the separation of powers:* that competing power centres can realistically endure without converging.

Let us deal with each of these in turn. The myth of the stateless society permeates the two competing ideologies of the Twentieth Century—liberalism and socialism—at their extreme ends in anarcho-libertarianism (whether left or right) and communism. Mosca and Michels demonstrate that this is fundamentally wrongheaded because minority organisation always prevails from the level of a tribe to the level of global government. Humans are, simply put, the political animal and what is called 'the state' is simply the fact that there must be the political function in any society.

The second myth that the state is separate from its laws and institutions is shown to be false by Carl Schmitt who demonstrates that, despite liberal pipedreams, there is no escape from the political. Even though the cloak of neutral or scientific language can be used to mask the ideological content, every institution will bear the mark of the dominant political formula which acts as a kind of theological holy writ. If the political formula is 'equality, diversity and inclusion', there can be no official bodies or laws that do not conform to it. Samuel T. Francis shows that managerial elites will not stop their social transformations until all relics and vestiges of the old and despised bourgeois regime are replaced by the new religion at every level of culture down to your local museum. Paul Gottfried shows that this is even taken to the domain of science and medicine to the extent those who resist the political formula are diagnosed with mental disorders.

The third myth that the state and the economy could ever be separated—the myth of the free market—is the central ten-et of classical liberalism.[1] Bertrand de Jouvenel shows that since the political comes prior to any economy, the economy itself can never and will never escape politics. James Burnham shows that *laissez-faire* was simply the political formula of the capitalists who gained power in the nineteenth century but this, because of the practicalities of mass and scale, gave way to managerialism and the fusion of corporate interests and the state. We have seen how even the economy in the managerial state is a top-down process: the consumer is not sovereign; despite the slogans, the managerial class use the roles of executives at large corporations and financial institutions to set directives and mission statements for the foreseeable time horizon. The reason organizations such as the UN and the World Economic Forum can announce their visions for 'Agenda 2030' is because the economy itself is managed.

The fourth myth is that there is a 'separation of powers' in a liberal democracy, which is to say that there are 'checks and balances' between the various branches of government. This is largely collapsed by the incisive analysis of Schmitt and the process of power's tendency to seek to conquer 'feudal castles' identified by Jouvenel. It is worth noting that at least three of the thinkers covered—Mosca, Burnham and Jouvenel himself—favour a system by which centralisation or the convergence of power centres is held in a kind of equilibrium through a constant struggle, even if in practice they recognise the extreme difficulty of achieving this.

While it appears that populism largely failed—not because it was not supported by the masses but because of political naïvety—that does not mean a circulation of the elites is not due. As the lies and manipulations of the managerial regime become more and more visible to a public that has become widely sceptical of our current globalist elites and the system that supports them, agitation for significant change will

1   See my own articulation of this idea in a book-length study: Neema Parvini, *The Defenders of Liberty: Human Nature, Individualism and Property Rights* (New York and London: Palgrave Macmillan, 2020).

continue apace. Attempts to maintain official narratives and maintain free and fair elections will become more difficult. It strikes me that the system then faces many possible points of failure which include:

1. De facto balkanization.
2. The need to for more explicit coercion and the use of force.
3. A 'high-low middle mechanism' whereby national governments become 'the middle' while supra-national globalist governance structures become the high and local regions become the middle.
4. Bioleninism, or in other words, degradation of the elites and exclusion of people of superior skills and talents, causes the ruling class to become complacent and / or inept.
5. Eclipse by foreign powers.

At the time of writing, we are seeing all five of these things in their nascent state. The political pressure from the public on elected leaders—due to the sheer unpopularity of the policies enacted—may eventually cause them to break decisively with globalist elites. This remains *likely* so long as nations maintain standing armies. Strong indications in France and elsewhere seem to make it almost inevitable that there will at least be a nominal struggle for national sovereignty against globalist overreach—the political capital spent on the COVID-19 pandemic will exacerbate this especially given the economic hardship it seems to be bringing. European populations may have a stated preference to achieve 'net zero carbon' by 2030, but in practice it is extremely unlikely that elites will be able to push ahead with their utopian visions without violent protest. As the situation worsens, people will become more serious and organised having learned from the populist experiences between 2016 and 2020. Elites, of course, always have an option to reverse course in a bid to reverse these trends, but one suspects that they believe their own visions with a missionary zeal. Even if they do not, the will to power is such that their lust for ever greater control will not let up until power is *taken* from them by a better organised elite with a political formula better suited to the populations they are supposed to serve. I strongly doubt that this new elite—when they emerge, whether by democratic means or otherwise—will be able to break decisively enough from liberal and democratic myths to do what is necessary to keep Western nations from experiencing certain disaster in the future. However, after decades of chronic mismanagement from the current 'managers', perhaps all we can hope for is a vaguely sensible replacement for a few years whose interests will be closer to those of 'the people'.

BIBLIOGRAPHY

Adorno, Theordor W., *The Authoritarian Personality* (New York: Harper & Brothers, 1950).

Albertoni, Ettore A., *Mosca and the Theory of Elitism*, trans. Paul Goodrick (Oxford: Blackwell, 1987).

Althusser, Louis, *Lenin and Philosophy and Other Essays*, trans. Ben Brewster (1971; New York: Monthly Review Press, 2001).

Amanpour, Christiane, 'Blair: Britain's Political Relationship with America Isn't Strong Anymore', *CNN* (22 January 2022): https://edition.cnn.com/videos/tv/2022/01/21/amanpour-tony-blair-future-of-britain-ukraine.cnn.

Arendt, Hannah, *The Origins of Totalitarianism* (1951; New York and London: Penguin, 2017).

Bartholomew, James, 'The Awful Rise of "Virtue Signalling"', *The Spectator* (April 18, 2015): https://www.spectator.co.uk/2015/04/hating-the-daily-mail-is-a-substitute-for-doing-good/.

Barr, Alistair, 'Mozilla CEO Brendan Eich Steps Down', *The Wall Street Journal* (3 April 2014): https://www.wsj.com/articles/mozilla-ceo-brendan-eich-to-step-down-1396554132.

Beetham, David, 'Michels and His Critics', *European Journal of*

Sociology, 22:1 (January 1981).

Bellamy, Richard, *Modern Italian Social Theory* (Oxford: Blackwell, 1987).

Benoist, Alain de, *The View from the Right*, 3 vols (1977; London: Arktos, 2018).

——, *Carl Schmitt Today: Terrorism, 'Just War' and the State of Emergency* (London: Arktos Media, 2013).

Bernays, Edward, *Propaganda* (1928; New York: Ig Publishing, 2005).

——, *Public Relations* (Norman, OK: University of Oklahoma Press, 1952).

Blinder, Scott, and Lindsay Richards, 'UK Public Opinion toward Immigration: Overall Attitudes and Level of Concern', *The Migration Observatory* (20 January 2020): https://migrationobservatory.ox.ac.uk/resources/briefings/uk-public-opinion-toward-immigration-overall-attitudes-and-level-of-concern/.

Bond, C. A., *Nemesis: The Jouvenelian vs. The Liberal Model of Human Orders* (Perth: Imperium Press, 2019).

Bottomore, Tom, *Elites and Society*, 2nd edn (1964; New York and London: Routledge, 1993).

Breuninger, Kevin, and Dan Mangan, 'WikiLeaks' Julian Assange charged with 17 new criminal counts, including violating Espionage Act', *CNBC* (23 May 2019): https://www.cnbc.com/2019/05/23/wikileaks-co-founder-julian-assange-charged-with-17-new-criminal-counts.html.

Brennan Center for Justice, 'A Guide to Emergency Powers and Their Use' (24 April 2020): https://www.brennancenter.org/our-work/research-reports/guide-emergency-powers-and-their-use.

Burnham, James, *The Managerial Revolution* (1941; Westport, CN: Greenwood Press, 1972).

——, *The Machiavellians: Defenders of Freedom* (London: Putnam, 1943).

———. 'Managing the Managers', *Challenge*, 8:8 (May 1960), 18-23.

———, *Suicide of the West: An Essay on the Meaning and Destiny of Liberalism* (New York: John Day Company, 1964).

Cassinelli, C.W., 'The Law of Oligarchy', *The American Political Science Review*, 47:3 (September 1957), 773-84.

Cialdini, Robert B., *Influence: The Psychology of Persuasion* (1984; New York: William Morrow, 2007).

Ciampini, Gabriele, 'Is Bertrand de Jouvenel only a Liberal Philosopher? The Relations between His Political Thought with the Twentieth Century Sociological Thought', *International Journal of Social Science and Humanity*, 3:5 (September 2013), 448-52.

———, 'The Elitism of Bertrand de Jouvenel: A Reinterpretation of Jouvenel's Political Theory Through the Elite Theory', *Academic Journal of Interdisciplinary Studies*, 2:21 (October 2013), 15-23.

Coughlin, Sean, 'Students Face Tuition Fees Rising to £9,000', *BBC News* (3 November 2010): https://www.bbc.co.uk/news/education-11677862.

Dalberg-Acton, John Emerich Edward, 'Acton-Creighton Correspondence', in *Essays on Freedom and Power*, ed. Gertrude Himmelfarb (Glencoe, IL: The Free Press, 1948).

Debunk the Flunk with Dr Wilson, 'Robert Malone Goes Full Anti-Science on Joe Rogan's Podcast', *YouTube* (5 January 2022): https://www.youtube.com/watch?v=xjsz-VOfG_wo.

Dreher, Rod, 'Nation First, Conservatism Second', *The American Conservative* (19 January 2016): https://www.theamericanconservative.com/dreher/nationalism-conservatism-trump-samuel-francis/.

Drochon, Hugo, 'Robert Michels, The Iron Law of Oligarchy

and Dynamic Democracy', *Constellations* 27 (2020), 185-98.

Dylan, Bob, 'Man of Peace', on *Infidels* (New York: Columbia Records, 1983).

'Edinburgh University renames David Hume Tower over 'racist' views', *BBC News* (13 September 2020): https://www.bbc.co.uk/news/uk-scotland-edinburgh-east-fife-54138247.

Egan, Matt, 'Video Game CEO is Out After Praising Texas Abortion Law', *CNN* (8 September 2021): https://edition.cnn.com/2021/09/07/business/tripwire-ceo-texas-abortion-law/index.html.

Ewen, Stuart, *Captains of Consciousness: Advertising and the Social Roots of the Consumer Culture* (New York: McGraw-Hill Book Company, 1976).

Femia, Joseph V., *Against the Masses: Varieties of Anti-Democratic Thought since the French Revolution* (Oxford: Oxford University Press, 2001).

Ferrarotti, Franco, 'The Italian Context: Pareto and Mosca', in *Pareto and Mosca*, ed. James H. Meisel (Englewood Cliffs, NJ: Prentice-Hall, 1965).

Fink, Larry, 'Larry Fink's 2022 Letter to CEOs: The Power of Capitalism', *Blackrock* (January 2022): https://www.blackrock.com/corporate/investor-relations/larry-fink-ceo-letter.

Finocchiaro, Maurice A., *Beyond Right and Left: Democratic Elitism in Mosca and Gramsci* (New Haven, MA: Yale University Press, 1999).

Foucault, Michel, *Madness and Civilization*, trans. Richard Howard (1961; New York and London: Routledge, 2010).

Francis, Samuel T., *Thinkers of our Time: James Burnham* (1984; London: The Claridge Press, 1999).

——, 'Anarcho-Tyranny—Where Multiculturalism Leads',

VDare (December 12, 2004): https://vdare.com/articles/ anarcho-tyranny-where-multiculturalism-leads.

——, *Beautiful Losers: Essays on the Failure of American Conservativism* (Columbia, MI: University of Missouri Press, 1994).

——, *Leviathan and Its Enemies* (Arlington, VA: Washing Summit Publishers, 2016).

Gilens, Martin, and Benjamin I. Page, 'Testing Theories of American Politics: Elites, Interest Groups, and Average Citizens', *Perspectives on Politics*, 12:3 (September 2014), 564-81.

Goldberg, Jonah, *Liberal Fascism: The Secret History of the Left from Mussolini to the Politics of Meaning* (New York and London: Penguin, 2009).

Gottfried, Paul, *Carl Schmitt: Politics and Theory* (New York: Greenwood Press, 1990).

——, *After Liberalism: Mass Democracy in the Managerial State* (Princeton, NJ: Princeton University Press, 1999).

——, 'The Black-Jewish Alliance', *Academic Questions*, 14:3 (Summer 2001), 6-7.

——, *Multiculturalism and The Politics of Guilt: Toward a Secular Theocracy* (Columbia, MI: University of Missouri Press, 2002).

——, *Fascism: The Career of a Concept* (Ithaca, IL: Northern Illinois University Press, 2017).

——, 'The Frankfurt School and Cultural Marxism', *American Thinker* (12 January 2018): https://www.americanthinker.com/articles/2018/01/the_frankfurt_school_and_cultural_marxism.html.

——, *Antifascism: The Course of a Crusade* (Ithaca, IL: Northern Illinois University Press, 2021).

Gottfried, Paul E. and Richard B. Spencer, (eds), *The Great Purge* (Arlington, VA: Washington Summit Publishers,

2015).

Gregor, A. James, *The Fascist Persuasion in Radical Politics* (Princeton, NJ: Princeton University Press, 1974).

Haidt, Jonathan, *The Righteous Mind: Why Good People Are Divided by Religion and Politics* (New York: Random House, 2012).

Hands, Gordon, 'Roberto Michels and the Study of Political Parties', *British Journal of Political Science*, 1:2 (April 1971), 155–72.

Heilman, Zack, 'CNN Accidentally Admits Their 'News' Isn't Working, People Are Just Living Their Lives, Ignoring Us', *Red Voice Media* (10 January 2022): https://www.redvoice-media.com/2022/01/cnn-accidentally-admits-their-news-isnt-working-people-are-just-living-their-lives-ignoring-us/.

Higley, John, 'Elite Theory and Elites', in *Handbook of Politics: State and Society in Global Perspective*, ed. Kevin T. Leicht and J. Craig Jenkins (New York: Springer, 2010).

Hook, Sidney, 'On James Burnham's *The Machiavellians*', *Society*, 25 (March 1988), 68–70.

Howard, Scott, *The Transgender Industrial Complex* (Quakertown, PA: Antelope Hill, 2020).

Hughes, H. Stuart, *Consciousness and Society* (Brighton: The Harvester Press, 1979).

Hume, David, *A Treatise of Human Nature* (1739; New York: Dover Publications, 2003).

——, *An Enquiry Concerning the Principles of Morals*, ed. J.B. Schneewind (1751; Indianapolis, IN: Hackett Publishing, 1983).

Jouvenel, Bertrand de, *On Power: The Natural History of Its Growth*, trans. J.F. Huntington (1945; Minneapolis, MN: Liberty Fund, 1993).

Kahneman, Daniel, *Thinking Fast and Slow* (New York and London: Penguin, 2011).

Kampmark, Binoy, 'The First Neo-conservative: James Burnham and the Origins of a Movement', *Review of International Studies*, 37:4 (2011), 1885-1907.

Kassam, Raheem, *No Go Zones: How Sharia Law Is Coming to a Neighborhood Near You* (Washington, DC: Regnery, 2017).

Kurtz, Howard, 'Washington Times Clips Its Right Wing', *The Washington Post* (October, 1995): https://www.washingtonpost.com/archive/lifestyle/1995/10/19/washington-times-clips-its-right-wing/dd009c93-883b-446c-bbbf-94c0a0570a1a/.

Kennedy, Ellen, 'Carl Schmitt and the Frankfurt School', *Telos*, 71 (March 1987), 37-66.

Lasch, Christopher, *The True and Only Heaven: Progress and Its Critics* (New York: W. W. Norton, 1991).

Lasswell, Harold D., and C. Easton Rothwell, *The Comparative Study of Elites* (Stanford, CA: Stanford University Press, 1952).

Le Bon, Gustave, *The Crowd: A Study of the Popular Mind* (1897; Greenville, SC: Traders Press, 1994).

Lippmann, Walter, *Public Opinion* (New York: Harcourt, Brace & Co.: 1922).

——, *The Phantom Public* (1927; New York: Routledge, 2017).

Machiavelli, Niccolò, *Discourses on Livy*, trans. Harvey C. Mansfield and Nathan Tarcov (1517; Chicago: University of Chicago Press, 1996

Mahoney, Daniel J., *Betrand de Jouvenel* (Wilmington, DE: ISI Books, 2005).

Manheim, Karl, *Ideology and Utopia* (London: Routledge & Kegan Paul, 1936).

May, John D., 'Democracy, Organization, Michels', *The American Political Science Review*, 59:2 (June 1965), 417–29.

McCallen, Scott, 'Over 7,000 Affidavits Delivered to Michigan Lawmakers Claim Election Fraud', *Washington Examiner* (18 June 2021): https://www.washingtonexaminer.com/politics/over-7-000-affidavits-delivered-to-michigan-lawmakers-claim-election-fraud.

Meisel, James H., *The Myth of the Ruling Class: Gaetano Mosca and the Elite* (Ann Arbor, MI: University of Michigan Press, 1962).

Michels, Robert, *Political Parties: A Sociology of the Oligarchical Tendencies of Modern Democracy* (1915; New York: The Free Press, 1962).

Mills, C. Wright, *The Power Elite* (1956; Oxford: Oxford University Press, 2000).

Moldbug, Mencius, *A Gentle Introduction to Unqualified Reservations* (Unqualified Reservations: 2015).

Mosca, Gaetano, *The Ruling Class*, ed. Arthur Livingston, trans. Hannah D. Khan (1895; New York: McGraw-Hill, 1939).

———, *A Short History of Political Philosophy*, trans. by Sondra Z. Koff (1933; New York: Thomas Cromwell, 1972).

Mouffe (ed.), Chantelle, *The Challenge of Carl Schmitt* (New York and London: Verso, 1999).

Ohana, David. 'Carl Schmitt's Legal Fascism', *Politics, Religion & Ideology*, 20:3 (2019), 1-28.

O'Neil, Daniel J., 'The Political Philosophy of James Burnham', *International Journal of Social Economics,* 21 (1994), 141-52.

Orwell, George, *Essays* (New York: Everyman's Library, 2002).

Palmer, Ewan, 'Papa John's Founder John Schnatter Says

Board Conspired to Oust Him, Vows "Day of Reckoning Will Come"', *Newsweek* (26 November, 2019): https://www.newsweek.com/papa-johns-john-schnatter-interview-1474073.

Pape, Robert A., '21 Million Americans say Biden is "Illegitimate" and Trump should be Restored by Violence, Survey Finds', *Opinion Today* (21 September 2021): https://opiniontoday.com/2021/09/23/21-million-americans-say-biden-is-illegitimate-and-trump-should-be-restored-by-violence-survey-finds/.

Pareto, Vilfredo, *The Mind and Society*, ed. Arthur Livingstone, trans. Andrew Bongiorno and Arthur Livingstone, 4 vols (1916; New York: Harcourt, Brace and Company, 1935).

——, *Compendium of General Sociology*, ed. Elisabeth Abbott (Minneapolis, MN: University of Minnesota Press, 1980).

Parry, Geraint, *Political Elites* (London: George Allen and Unwin, 1971).

Parvini, Neema, *Shakespeare and Cognition: Thinking Fast and Slow through Character* (New York and London: Palgrave Macmillan, 2015).

——, *Shakespeare's Moral Compass* (Edinburgh: Edinburgh University Press, 2018).

——, *The Defenders of Liberty: Human Nature, Individualism, and Property Rights* (New York and London: Palgrave Macmillan, 2020).

Pengelly, Martin, 'One in Three Americans Say Violence Against the Government is Justified—Poll', *The Guardian* (2 January 2022): https://www.theguardian.com/us-news/2022/jan/02/one-three-americans-violence-government-justified-poll.

Pierce, Roy, *Contemporary French Political Thought* (Oxford: Oxford University Press, 1966).

Podhoretz, Norman, *World War IV: The Long Struggle Against*

Islamofascism (New York: Doubleday, 2007).

Putnam, Robert D., *The Comparative Study of Political Elites* (Englewood Cliffs, NJ: Prentice-Hall, 1976).

Rasch, William, *Carl Schmitt: State and Society* (New York and London: Rowman & Littlefied, 2019).

Reaves, R.B., 'Orwell's "Second Thoughts on James Burnham" and *1984*, *College Literature*, 11:1 (1984), 13-21.

Rhodes, Carl, *Woke Capitalism: How Corporate Morality is Sabotaging Democracy* (Bristol: Bristol University Press, 2022).

Roth, Carol, 'The Greatest Transfer of Wealth From the Middle Class to the Elites in History', *Brownstone Institute* (1 November 2021): https://brownstone.org/articles/the-greatest-transfer-of-wealth-from-the-middle-class-to-the-elites-in-history/.

Russ, Hilary, and Nivedita Balu, 'Beyond Meat Loss Exceeds Forecasts on Higher Costs, Slow Restaurant Sales', *Reuters* (6 May 2021), ' https://www.reuters.com/business/retail-consumer/beyond-meat-quarterly-revenue-misses-estimates-2021-05-06/.

Sales, Dan, 'JK Rowling is Cancelled Again: Performing Arts School Drops Harry Potter Author's name from House over Her Views on Transgender Rights', *Daily Mail* (4 January 2022): https://www.dailymail.co.uk/news/article-10367133/JK-Rowling-cancelled-Performing-arts-school-drops-Harry-Potter-author-transgender-row.html.

Schmitt, Carl, *Political Theology: Four Chapters on the Concept of Sovereignty*, trans. George Schwab (1922; Chicago, IL: University of Chicago Press, 2005).

——, *The Concept of the Political*, trans. George Schwab (1932; Chicago, IL: University of Chicago Press, 2007).

——, *The Tyranny of Values*, ed. and trans. Simona Draghici (1967; Washington, D.C.: Plutarch Press, 1996).

——, *The Sovereign Collection*, trans C.J. Miller (Quakertown, PA: Antelope Hill Publishing, 2020).

Schueurman, Bill. 'Carl Schmitt and the Nazis', *German, Politics and Society*, 23 (Summer 1991), 71-79.

Schwab, George, *The Challenge of the Exception: An Introduction to the Political Ideas of Carl Schmitt Between 1921 and 1936* (1970; New York: Greenwood Press, 1989).

Schupmann, Benjamin A., *Carl Schmitt's State and Constitutional Theory: A Critical Analysis* (Oxford: Oxford University Press, 2017).

Setty, Madhava, 'Rogan and Malone: Most Important Interview of Our Time?', *The Defender* (4 January 2022): https://childrenshealthdefense.org/defender/joe-rogan-robert-malone-interview-covid-vaccine/.

Shesol, Jeff, *Supreme Power: Franklin Roosevelt vs. The Supreme Court* (New York: W.W. Norton, 2010).

Shreeve-McGiffen, Maximillian, 'The Coronavirus Act 2020: Unprecedented Powers, But Are They Necessary?', *The Oxford University Undergraduate Law Journal* (7 May 2020): https://www.law.ox.ac.uk/ouulj/blog/2020/05/coronavirus-act-2020-unprecedented-powers-are-they-necessary.

Simpson, George, 'JK Rowling's "Prominent Absence' from Harry Potter Reunion "like not inviting The Queen"', *Daily Express* (29 December 2021): https://www.express.co.uk/entertainment/films/1542583/JK-Rowling-absence-Harry-Potter-reunion-Return-to-Hogwarts-reviews.

Slevin, Carl, 'Social Change and Human Values: A Study of the Thought of Bertrand de Jouvenel', *Political Studies*, 19:1 (March 1971), 49-62.

Smith, Adam, *The Theory of Moral Sentiments*, ed. Ryan Patrick Henley (1759; New York and London: Penguin, 2010).

Smith, Blake, 'Liberalism for Losers: Carl Schmitt's "The Tyranny of Values"', *American Affairs*, 5.1 (Spring 2021): https://americanaffairsjournal.org/2021/02/liberalism-for-losers-carl-schmitts-the-tyranny-of-values/.

Sorel, Georges, *Reflections on Violence*, trans. T. E. Hulme, ed. Jeremy Jennings (1908; Cambridge University Press, 1999).

Sorensen, Charles E., *My Forty Years with Ford* (New York: Norton, 1956).

Sowell, Thomas, *A Conflict of Visions: Ideological Origins of Political Struggles*, rev. ed. (1987; New York: Basic Books, 2007).

Spandrell, 'Leninism and Bioleninism', *Bloody Shovel 3* (21 January 2018): https://spandrell.com/2017/11/14/biological-leninism/.

Spengler, Oswald, *The Decline of the West*, trans. Charles Francis Atkinson (1918-22; London: George Allen & Unwin, 1961).

——, *The Hour of Decision: Germany and World-Historical Evolution* (1934; Honolulu, HI: University Press of the Pacific, 2002).

Spencer, Herbert, *The Man versus The State* (1884; Indianapolis, IN: Liberty Fund, 1982).

Spocchia, Gino, 'No Academic Credibility': Experts Debunk Mass Psychosis Covid theory Floated by Doctor on Joe Rogan Podcast', *The Independent* (10 January 2022): https://www.independent.co.uk/news/world/americas/covid-psychosis-theory-joe-rogan-b1989552.html.

Swaine, Jon, 'Peter Mandelson profile: The Prince of Darkness Returns', *Daily Telegraph* (3 October 2008): https://www.telegraph.co.uk/news/politics/labour/3127802/Peter-Mandelson-profile-The-Prince-of-Darkness-returns.html.

Thomas Szasz, *Law, Liberty and Psychiatry* (New York: Macmillan, 1963).

——, *The Myth of Mental Illness* (New York: Harper & Row, 1961).

——, *Psychiatric Justice* (New York: Macmillan, 1965).

Talmon, J.L., *The Origins of Totalitarian Democracy* (London: Secker and Warburg, 1952).

Thaler, Shannon, 'YouTube and Twitter Delete Joe Rogan Interview with Scientist who Helped Invent mRNA Vaccines', *Daily Mail* (3 January, 2022): https://www.dailymail.co.uk/news/article-10364679/YouTube-Twitter-delete-Joe-Rogan-interview-scientist-helped-invent-MRNA-vaccines.html.

The Joe Rogan Experience, '#1757—Dr Robert Malone, MD' (31 December 2021): https://open.spotify.com/episode/3SCsueX2bZdbEzRtKOCEyT.

Ulmen, G.L., and Paul Piccone, 'Introduction to Carl Schmitt', *Telos*, 72 (June 1987), 3-14.

UK Cabinet Office, 'Written Ministerial Statement on Unconscious Bias Training', *Gov.uk* (17 December 2020): https://www.gov.uk/government/news/written-ministerial-statement-on-unconscious-bias-training.

United States v. Julian Paul Assange, Criminal No. 1:18-cr-1 11 (CMH): https://www.justice.gov/opa/press-release/file/1153486/download?utm_medium=email&utm_source=govdelivery/.

Vazquez, Maegan, 'George W. Bush: Bigotry and White Supremacy are "Blasphemy" against the American Creed (19 October 2017): https://edition.cnn.com/2017/10/19/politics/bush-freedom-event/index.html.

Villarreal, Daniel, 'RNC Chair Says People Have Come Forward With 11,000 Voter Fraud Claims', *Newsweek* (11 November 2020): https://www.newsweek.com/rnc-chair-says-11000-people-have-come-forward-voter-fraud-claims-1546546.

Weise, Karen, 'Amazon's Profit Soars 220 Percent as Pandemic Drives Shopping Online', *New York Times* (29 April 2021): https://www.nytimes.com/2021/04/29/technology/amazons-profits-triple.html.

World Economic Forum, *The Global Risks Report 2022* (Davos: World Economic Forum, 2022).

Wooster, Martin Morse, *The Great Philanthropists and the Problem of 'Donor Intent'*, 3rd edn (1998; Washington, DC: Capital Research Center, 2007).

Yarvin, Curtis, 'The Clear Pill, Part 1 of 5: The Four-Stroke Regime', *The American Mind* (27 September 2019): https://americanmind.org/salvo/the-clear-pill-part-1-of-5-the-four-stroke-regime/.

INDEX

Milton Keynes UK
Ingram Content Group UK Ltd.
UKHW020648211123
432973UK00009B/167